Quebecq

Onjure ofte Assarenwe

Schoen Vlack land

Marquaa Kill

taFenay

Schanatissa

Canagero

t'Ounontego

Mackwaas

t'Fort Orangie

COLO

Vsschersboec

d'Oude Rei

Berren Eylant

Hoppe Eylant

Walvis Eylant

NYE

t'Greynbos

Steurhoeck

Mabicans Eylant

WYCK

Marten Gerritsoons Eylant

Sterten Rack

Noten boeck

t'Vaste Rack

Brackers Rock

Horika

Mr. Pinsers handel

bays

RENSELAERS

Hinnenhoeck

Ian Blaisiersde

Klaverack

Kats Kill

Nawaas

Land van Kats Kill

NEDER

Roeloff Iansoons

Kill

LAND

innessinck ofte

ndt van Baeham

Hooge Land

van Esopus

Wieskottine

Groote Esopus R.

Cleyne Esopus

lande wits Eylant

Magdalen Eylant

Slypsteen Eylant

Sequins

he pinaikonck

Waranawankongs

Kaes Eylant

Meerch konck

Macharienkonck

Wap pinges

Tame Kanut

Wappinges

Kill

Waoranecks

Rodenberghs

River

Makimanes

Qu irepeys

l'Schichte

Wacki

Narratschoen

Vischer Ruch

Clinkers

Bergh

Verdrietigehoeck

Colonie

VAN

Tappaans

DE HEER NEDER

Schoenareyne

Bosch

Nodi Peem

Pasqunshuck

Keskistkonck

Kestaubunck

Sinsing

Alipkonck

Wickquaskick

Wecke

Tachami

Yauischiestawick

Pechquenakonck

Siwanoys

Quyropey

Roodenbergh

Keuhaven

Milford

Betotalet

Venosse Rak

Hoog

t'Veck R. Rack

Sintmaerkers Rack

Haverstroo

Ipoena

Saeck

Hellgat

Beluck

Greenbis

a quapod

Stamfort

Strotfort

De Keer

Ian Wittems

Eylant

Archipelago

HORST

Pechquakeck

Nieuw Amsterdam

Rivier

achter Kol

Sanhicans

Manhattans

Oost Rivier

Mispat

Breuckelen

Vlissinghen

Amersfoert

Lange Eylant alias

Gebocken

landt

Matouwaes

Sickete Wachly

S. Holt

Greenwick

Graveson

Haemstee

Gromme

Lucus

Bariton

Godyns Bay

Port May of

Magockqueshou

Noe Sinck

Verhulsten Eylant

Wickweck

gos

Matovancons

Aquauacu oques

Kemkoekes

Aruysmenhoeck

Mispennick

Timmerk

Ermomex

t'Fort Nassou

Brakskonck

Varkens Kill

Arme-waick

Amucaronck

Naeranis Karonck

t'Fort Elsenburgh

Naraticons

Se Swapois

Barndegat

Everhaven

al. Boye haven

Barndegat

Groote Rivier a

Sant Paint of

Godyns Punt

Bedenburghs

hoeck

Manhattins R.

Noort Rivier

Montaigne Rivier

Maarts Rivier

MAR DEL

NORT

NIEUW AMSTERDAM

opt Eylant Manhattans

Exploring Historic Dutch New York

New York City, Hudson Valley, New Jersey, and Delaware

Gajus Scheltema and Heleen Westerhuijs, editors

MUSEUM OF THE CITY OF NEW YORK

DOVER PUBLICATIONS

Copyright

Bibliographical Note

*Exploring Historic Dutch New York: New York City * Hudson Valley * New Jersey * Delaware*, first published in 2011, is a new work, published jointly by the Museum of the City of New York and Dover Publications, Inc.

International Standard Book Number

ISBN-13: 978-0-486-48637-6
ISBN-10: 0-486-48637-0

Manufactured in the United States by Courier Corporation
48637001
www.doverpublications.com

TITLE PAGE: Map of New Netherland, 1650s. This map is from Adriaen van der Donck's book, *Beschryvinge van Nieuw-Nederlant (ghelijck het tegenwoordigh in staet is)* (Description of New Netherland).

THIS PUBLICATION WAS MADE POSSIBLE BY

CITCO

MAJOR SPONSORSHIP WAS ALSO PROVIDED BY

Deloitte.

ADDITIONAL SUPPORT HAS BEEN RECEIVED FROM

Atlantic Investment Management
Sybase Inc.
Van Dyk Baler Corp.
Rosabianca & Associates, PLLC
Hogan Lovells
Alston + Bird LLP
Furthermore: A Program of the J.M. Kaplan Fund
Ted Moudis
The Society of Daughters of Holland Dames

Foreword

The year 2009, in which we celebrated the 400th anniversary of Henry Hudson's voyage across the Atlantic, served as a wonderful opportunity for the Museum of the City of New York to consider New YorkÐs Dutch heritage. In the exhibition *Amsterdam/New Amsterdam: The Worlds of Henry Hudson,* the epiphany was that there is much "Dutch" in the character of the city today. The Dutch established the colony of New Netherland and welcomed ambitious people of all kinds—Walloons, Huguenots, Germans, French, English, and Jews—who would help make it profitable. By 1643 there were 18 languages spoken in New Amsterdam.

New Netherland was a very different place from neighboring colonies. Its uncommon diversity, focus on commerce, and contentious politics seeded the character of this mid-Atlantic region in the 21st century. Thus, the Museum is happy to participate in a project that is essentially an outgrowth of the 400th anniversary celebration—a guidebook that documents the surviving tangible elements of the Dutch past in present-day New York, New Jersey, and parts of Delaware. As the pages of this book show, the legacy of this region's Dutch origins is still evident, not only in place names and historic sites, but most visibly in the distinctive domestic architecture of surviving Dutch colonial buildings and adaptations of Dutch styles. Examples of gambrel roofs, step gables, and Dutch split doors can be seen today, along with the mid-19th-century Dutch Colonial Revival style. This book can be your guide to this fascinating architectural legacy.

Gajus Scheltema conceived of this book and, with his co-editor, Heleen Westerhuijs, developed the concept. Roald Smeets of the Citco Group of Companies, who co-chaired the Museum's 2009 exhibition *Amsterdam/New Amsterdam: The Worlds of Henry Hudson,* was the catalyst for this ambitious project and the driving force throughout its creation.

OPPOSITE: Van Dusen House, Claverack (detail). Note the pigeon holes, and weaved brick courses.

The Museum is also grateful for the generosity of Evenson Best LLC, whose co-founder, Vernon Evenson, is a Museum trustee; Deloitte; Alexander Roepers of Atlantic Investment Management, who also co-chaired the *Amsterdam/New Amsterdam* exhibition; Van Dyk Baler Corp.; Sybase; Rosabianca & Associates, PLLC; Hogan Lovells; Furthermore, a program of the J.M. Kaplan Fund; Alston+Bird LLP; Ted Moudis; and The Society of Daughters of Holland Dames.

Paul Carlos and Kari Johanesen of Pure+Applied have created a marvelous design for the book. Dr. Sarah Henry and Kathleen Benson, with the assistance of intern Grace-Yvette Gemmel, have kept all the parts of the project moving forward. Natalie Shivers edited the texts, Gwen Smith created the illustration program, and Henk van Assen and Jiashan Wu produced the maps.

I hope you will enjoy revisiting our region's Dutch past.

Susan Henshaw Jones
Ronay Menschel Director
Museum of the City of New York

Editors' Notes

The 400th anniversary of the famous voyage of Henry Hudson on his ship, the *Half Moon* (*Halve Maen*), was celebrated extensively in New York City and State in 2009. Hudson's exploration had led to the birth of the Dutch colony of New Netherland and its primary settlement, New Amsterdam, which lasted about half a century before the surrender to the British.

The NY400 festivities inspired—among many other events—over 30 English-language publications on the history of American-Dutch relations. At the time, however, we felt that one book was still to be written: a travel guide that would introduce a modern-day explorer to the Dutch legacy in New York, New Jersey and Delaware. *Exploring Historic Dutch New York* now attempts to meet that need.

We hope, of course, that this travel guide will be read and used by Americans and Dutch visitors alike. In particular, it should encourage New Yorkers and New Jerseyans to visit places they have never been before. The guide will also remind Americans of Dutch descent of their heritage and give Dutch tourists a sense of familiarity across the Atlantic.

As we started this project, the first question that came to mind was: how do you actually define something as "Dutch" in this part of the world? It turned out to be a complicated question, hard to answer in an academic sense, and even harder in the context of this travel guide. The colony of New Netherland was ethnically and linguistically diverse from its very beginning, and often, we realize, its "Dutchness" should be taken with quite a pinch of salt. This meant that, for example, the French-speaking Walloon and Huguenot legacies were to be included, as well as those of fellow settlers from different parts of Europe. Eighteenth-century houses often continued to be built in what is known as the "Dutch" tradition, but that architectural term is often debated among architectural historians. This guide will certainly reveal the diversity and richness of the "Dutch" legacy, which is sometimes only Dutch in its broader context. We could not afford to be purists in this respect, no more than the first settlers were!

This book also does not pretend to constitute an exhaustive list of all places "Dutch." Much is still to be discovered, and some sites proved to be less suited to the purposes of this travel guide. While we aimed at highlighting the legacy of the 17th century in general terms, we did not shy away from some more recent manifestations of "Dutch" heritage in this part of North America. We wanted to describe what we consider interesting to read about or worthwhile to visit. This, of course, is a subjective judgement of ours and should be treated as such.

Except in Lower Manhattan, the traces of Dutch heritage are often few and far between. We focused on the area that had been most intensively settled, from Schenectady and Albany in the north to the Delaware River in the south, from the Delaware Water Gap in the west to Long Island in the east, with New York City as its core. Most of the suggested tours require travel by private vehicle, and a tour could require several days to complete. The maps we have supplied are intended to orient readers to the relative locations of sites. They are not suitable for actual visits to the sites without the aid of more accurate local maps and/or GPS-based navigational tools.

The sites that we included are of varying cultural and historic interest—certainly for the European tourist, spoiled by a rich architectural legacy on the European continent. However, tucked away between modern developments, little gems can still be traced and enjoyed. Time and again we were surprised ourselves by what is left, and we hope you will share our excitement as you use this travel guide!

This book was a collective effort. We invited experts on specific subjects to contribute to chapters of the main text and/or to inserts. The quality of the travel guide is due to them, and inadvertent shortcomings are totally our responsibility as editors. Our contributors are acknowledged by name at the end of this book. We are proud to have been able to work together with all of those who shared their wisdom and passion for the many aspects of the Dutch legacy across the Atlantic. We thank them all!

Gajus Scheltema and Heleen Westerhuijs
New York, Spring 2011

Introduction

Russell Shorto

Everyone who reads history has the same secret wish: to go back there. If you are poring through Edward Gibbon's famous *Decline and Fall of the Roman Empire,* somewhere in your mind you are situating yourself among the consuls, citizens, and soldiers, wondering, were you somehow able actually to rub shoulders with them, just how vibrantly red the madder-dyed tunics would be, how the air would smell, what information the gaze of ancient eyes would transmit. Imagining past events is especially intriguing if the setting has been utterly transformed from what it once was. Surely no landscape of the present is so at odds with the past as Manhattan Island. When the Dutch colony of New Netherland was settled in the 1620s, with its capital of New Amsterdam at the southern tip of what the Indians called "*Manna Hatta,*" the island was a wilderness of oak-pine forest, red-maple swamp, marsh, pond, and meadow, rimmed by beaches and reed beds, alive with rattlesnakes, bears, and wolves.

To mentally step, therefore, from the urban intensity of New York today to the natural paradise it once was is surely one of the most exquisite adventures that history can offer. And, of course, New Netherland was not only a wilderness. Its Indian inhabitants had their complex cultures, and the colony itself—which stretched across much of the Middle Atlantic and encompassed all or parts of the future states of New York, New Jersey, Pennsylvania, Connecticut, and Delaware—was a purposeful settlement, which had an enormous influence not just on how New York would develop, but on the future United States and on the American identity. The Dutch who settled it—wedged between the English settlements of New England and Virginia—possessed Europe's only republic; they were a free-trading people; their home provinces, thanks in part to the flatness of the terrain (which made the land easy to invade or to flee to), had developed an official policy of tolerance to allow different peoples to coexist. These characteristics made the Dutch unique in Europe in the 17th century. When the settlers brought those characteristics with

Mr. and Mrs. Samuel Bayard, ca. 1644, by an unidentified painter

them to their New World colony, they evolved into something wholly new. If you simply took two of the main ingredients of the 17th-century Dutch Golden Age society—its tolerance and its proto-capitalist, free-trading sensibility—you would have something like a recipe for the growth of New York City.

In fact, once the English took over New Netherland and renamed its capital New York City, these characteristics stayed as part of its cultural structure. New Amsterdam's melting pot society (18 languages were being spoken in its few streets) turned into the multiethnic mix of New York. The city became colonial

America's immigrant focal point. And because New York became
what it did, the influence of New Netherland extended far beyond.
By the 19th century, when the great waves of immigrants reached
American shores, they first landed in large numbers in Manhattan's
mean streets. There they took in what was the legacy of the Dutch
colony: a teeming concentration of different ethnicities and faiths,
a mix of people all struggling to get ahead, fired by something
we now call upward mobility. As these newcomers breathed
this strange new air, they decided this new kind of society was
"America." In fact, it was New York, and it was New York because

formerly it had been New Netherland. But as those 19th-century immigrants moved from Manhattan westward to stake their own claims, they carried these seeds of 17th-century Dutch culture with them and planted the seeds in new soil—in the Great Plains, the Midwest, and the Pacific coast—and so, in time, they ensured that the new society was, indeed, America.

If, therefore, you could travel back in time and visit New Netherland, you would find yourself in proto-America: the country's first free-trading, immigrant society. You would also find yourself in a landscape out of Rembrandt: a place where men wore floppy, wide-brimmed hats; lace collars; and high leather boots. *Nieuw Amsterdam* (New Amsterdam), *Breuckelen,* and *Beverwijck* were villages of gabled houses, with a population of Dutch, French Huguenots, English, Germans, Swedish, Africans, and Indians. New Netherland was a place of rough adventurers; pious, God-fearing burghers; and farming families working with bent backs against the immensity of the landscape.

It is all gone, long gone. But traces remain. Some are preserved as historic houses or in museums. Other traces are in the shapes of the geography, the run of a street, the slope of a roofline, the tilt of a gravestone. And, of course, the traces are most evident in place names. From Brooklyn to the Bronx, from Harlem to Staten Island, from Cape May, New Jersey, to Rhode Island, the Dutch left names on the American landscape that still endure.

Most of those traces are not immediately apparent. The purpose of this volume is to bring them into focus. New Netherland is a curiously forgotten piece of our landscape and history—curious because it is simply bizarre that something so elemental to the American psyche could be so thoroughly expunged from our collective memory. Without New Netherland, would there be a Statue of Liberty? Would there have been an Ellis Island? Would the phrase "American melting pot" have come into being? American society today—free, democratic, multiethnic yet with the multiplicity of identities complementing rather than competing with a national identity—is almost a template for modern societies everywhere. It is an ideal that so many other places aspire to. And its roots are to be found here, in this volume. They may be found at places like the Zwaanendael Museum in Lewes, Delaware; the Hopper-Goetschius House in Upper Saddle River, New Jersey; the Old Huguenot Burial Ground in New

Old Huguenot Burial Ground and
French Church, New Paltz

Paltz, New York; or in Van Cortlandt Park in the Bronx. They
may be found in the street pattern of Lower Manhattan and along
the course of Broadway (or parts of it, anyway). They may be
found by car, by ferry, on foot, or, of course, simply by sitting in
a chair with an open book. Searching for those roots—trying to
will that lost world back into being—is a worthwhile endeavor. As
the great Dutch historian J.H. Huizinga once said, to understand
history, "we cannot do better than start from that mainspring of
all historical knowledge: our perpetual astonishment that the past
was once a living reality." And appreciating the living reality that
once existed informs, enriches, and maybe even ennobles our own.

A Short History of New Netherland

Jaap Jacobs

Dutch involvement in North America started with Henry Hudson's 1609 voyage on his ship, the *Half Moon* (*Halve Maen*). Employed by the Dutch East India Company, the English navigator set out in April of that year from Texel in the Dutch Republic to look for a passage to Asia north of Russia. He soon decided to try the northwestern route instead. Having reached the North American shore, he explored several inlets along the coast and entered the Upper New York Bay on September 11. After sailing what is now the Hudson River up to modern-day Albany, he returned to Europe, where word of his findings quickly spread. Dutch merchant companies, keen to take advantage of a profitable fur trade with the native inhabitants, soon sent ships to explore new waters and new economic opportunities along the American coast.

At first, the trade of these private merchant companies, including the newly established New Netherland Company, was of a seasonal nature. After a small fort (Fort Nassau) was built on the upper reaches of the Hudson River close to present-day Albany, trade continued on a more secure footing. Using the lower Hudson as a base, Dutch skippers like Adriaen Block, Cornelis Hendricksz, and Jacob Eelkens charted parts of the North American coast from the Delaware River to Cape Cod. The early trade patterns were initially continued when the Dutch West India Company (WIC) was founded in 1621. The WIC combined separate merchant companies into a single joint stock company, which obtained a monopoly over all Dutch trade and shipping across the Atlantic Ocean. The main aim was to finance the continuing war with Spain and Portugal through profits from trade. This "grand design" emphasized privateering against enemy shipping in the Caribbean Sea and attacks on Spanish and Portuguese colonies, such as Brazil. New Netherland was a minor concern for the WIC. Yet, within a few years, an important

OPPOSITE: *Manhattan, 1660* (detail) by L.F. Tantillo. A re-imagined view of New Amsterdam.

The Schaghen Letter, the first known document that mentions the sale of Manhattan Island to the Dutch by the Indians.

change occurred. English protests against the Dutch incursions on the American northeast coast, along with the wish to take over the commercial activities there from private merchants, prompted the WIC to send colonists in order to boost their territorial claims with settlements.

The exact chronology of events leading up to the founding of New Netherland is murky, as few relevant documents have survived. The first groups of colonists—mostly Walloons (French-speaking Protestants originating from the southern part of the

Low Countries, now Belgium)—probably arrived in 1624. They were dispersed around four trading posts, each with a fort: Fort Orange (later Albany) on the upper Hudson River; Burlington Island on the Delaware River; an undetermined location (probably Saybrook Point) on the mouth of the Connecticut River; and Governors Island (*Nooten Eylandt*). The colony was governed by a director, who represented the WIC as well as the highest governing body in the Dutch Republic, the States General (*Staten Generaal*). The director was assisted by a council of advisors, appointed by the Amsterdam chamber of the WIC. (The WIC was governed by five offices, called chambers, located in Amsterdam, Rotterdam, Hoorn, Middelburg, and Groningen). The WIC directors initially considered making Burlington Island the headquarters of their operations, but subsequently changed their minds and allowed local officials to choose a suitable location, suggesting the southern tip of Manhattan.

By September 1626 the Dutch had started building a fort on the southern tip of Manhattan—or *Manna Hatta,* the "hilly island," as the Native Americans called it—which had earlier been used as a pasture for livestock. The entire island was bought from the Native Americans for 60 guilders in merchandise while Pieter Minuit was director of New Netherland. On the whole, however, available information does not satisfy the modern desire to designate a specific year as the founding date of New York City.

After 1640 New Netherland gradually began to transform from a chain of trading posts into a settlement colony. In comparison with New England and Virginia, however, population growth was slow. This was partly due to the WIC's retention of its monopoly on the fur trade until 1640. After the company gave up its monopoly, immigration increased considerably, especially in the 1650s. Yet the development of New Netherland was always hampered by the prosperity of the Dutch Republic itself. Amsterdam in particular attracted fortune seekers from around Europe, few of whom were tempted to go overseas. The Dutch were even less likely to settle abroad and, if they did, the East Indies or Brazil offered better opportunities for getting rich quickly. As a result, half of New Netherland's settlers originated from European countries other than the Dutch Republic.

As the population increased, so did the administrative apparatus. When a sufficient number of colonists had settled in an area, the director and council often granted them a limited form of autonomy, including their own court of justice. The WIC also tried to stimulate growth of the settler population through the creation of patroonships, which granted governmental powers over large tracts of land to absentee landowners who would set up tenant farms at their own expense. By 1664 New Netherland was a settlement colony of 7,000–8,000 inhabitants, composed of New Amsterdam, 16 villages, and 2 patroonships. Most of the villages were concentrated on Long Island; others were located along the banks of the Hudson and Delaware Rivers. Areas further inland, such as in New Jersey, were mostly settled after 1664 when the English took over New Netherland.

Despite the population growth, colonists in New Netherland were thinly spread over a vast territory, and the colony was underpopulated in comparison with its neighbors. Pressure from the surrounding English colonists continued and eventually, in 1664, London sent a military force under Colonel Richard Nicolls to New Amsterdam to demand its surrender. Director General Petrus Stuyvesant was able to offer only a token defense, and New Netherland was quickly brought under English control. As the English takeover occurred in peacetime, it contributed to the outbreak of the Second Anglo-Dutch War (1665–1667). During subsequent negotiations leading to the Treaty of Breda in 1667, it was agreed that each country should keep the territories conquered during that war. This meant that the English retained control of former New Netherland, and the Dutch Republic remained in control of Surinam, which had been taken from the English in 1667.

In 1673, during the Third Anglo-Dutch War (1672–1674), New York was briefly recaptured by the Dutch and renamed New Orange. It was returned to the English under the terms of the Treaty of Westminster a year later. Half a century of Dutch rule on the North American continent had finally come to an end.

THE DUTCH SURRENDER NEW AMSTERDAM

The Dutch Surrender New Amsterdam, 1664,
an 1895 painting, depicting the capitulation of
the colony to the English by Director General
Petrus Stuyvesant.

MAP 1
Manhattan/ New Amsterdam
Downtown Manhattan

HUDSON RIVER

A

B

C

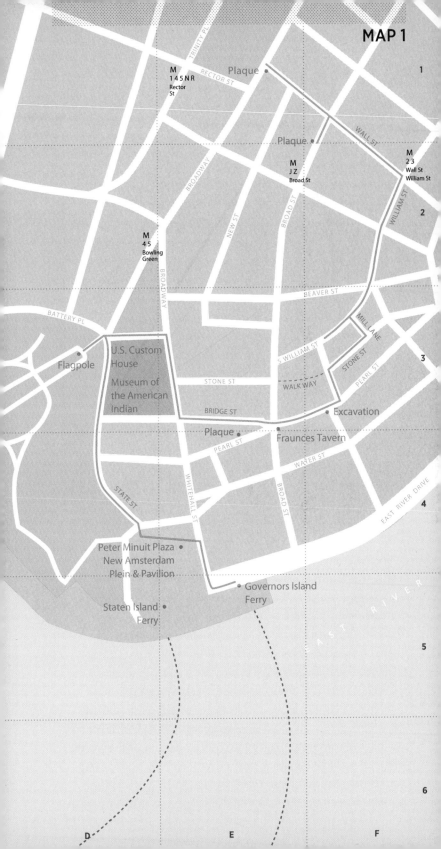

MAP 1

1

Plaque

M
1 4 5 N R
Rector
St

Plaque

WALL ST

BROADWAY

RECTOR ST

TRINITY PL

M
2 3
Wall St
William St

M
J Z
Broad St

2

NEW ST

BROAD ST

WILLIAM ST

M
4 5
Bowling
Green

BROADWAY

BEAVER ST

MILL LANE

3

S. WILLIAM ST

STONE ST

PEARL ST

U.S. Custom
House

Museum of
the American
Indian

STONE ST

WALKWAY

BRIDGE ST

Excavation

Flagpole

Plaque

Fraunces Tavern

PEARL ST

BATTERY PL

WATER ST

STATE ST

WHITEHALL ST

BROAD ST

EAST RIVER DRIVE

4

Peter Minuit Plaza
New Amsterdam
Plein & Pavilion

Governors Island
Ferry

Staten Island
Ferry

EAST   RIVER

5

6

D   E   F

Manhattan/
New Amsterdam

By late 1626 the Dutch had firmly settled on the island of Manhattan. With Fort Amsterdam as its center, they established a small trading post on the southern tip of the island. The village that surrounded Fort Amsterdam gradually developed into a small town that became the staple port and capital of New Netherland, replacing the earliest outposts on the Delaware, Hudson, and Connecticut Rivers. From only a couple of hundred settlers in the 1620s, the Dutch colony had reached a total population of 7,000–8,000 spread out over a wide area by the time of the English takeover in 1664. The city of "Amsterdam in New Netherland," as it was commonly called, then housed between 1,750 and 2,000 inhabitants, including 10–17 percent partly enslaved, partly freed African Americans. Among the colonists of European origin, about half had been born in the Dutch Republic. Many others originated in France, the German states, Scandinavia, and other European countries and had spent a number of years in Amsterdam or elsewhere in the Dutch Republic before emigrating to the New World. These included Huguenots and Walloons, French-speaking Protestants from France and Wallonia who had moved to the Dutch Republic. The majority of the elite, on the other hand, originated from the province of Holland. The public culture of the New Amsterdam elite was Dutch, with a few adaptations to the conditions of the New World.

Arriving colonists would sail past Coney Island (*Conijne Eylant*), through the Narrows between Staten Island (*Staten Eylant*) and Long Island (*'t Lange Eylant*), until the smaller islands in New York Bay came into sight: Liberty Island (*Bedloe's Eylant*), Ellis Island (*Oester Eylant*), and Governors Island (*Nooten Eylant*). The Hudson River was then commonly called North River (*Noordrivier*), a name for its southernmost part still in use by sailors. The ship would anchor on the East River (*Oostrivier*), within sight of the ferry to Brooklyn (*Breuckelen*), and sloops would transfer the new colonists and their cargo to the pier on Pearl Street (*Paerl Straet*). Along Pearl Street they would see the tavern-turned-city hall on the right and, on the left, the WIC warehouse, where all imported merchandise had to be cleared. Many of the older New Amsterdam houses were built of wood and resembled Dutch houses in the Waterland region north of Amsterdam.

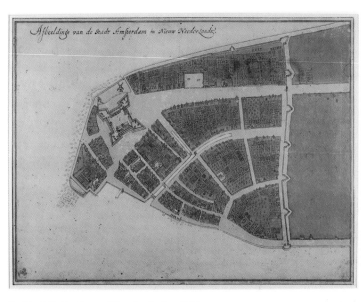

The "Castello Plan" map of New Amsterdam, 1660

Above the houses, the new arrivals would see Fort Amsterdam and, in the direction of the fort along Pearl Street, Petrus Stuyvesant's house on a little cape protruding into the East River. Turning right into the Marketfield (the *Marckvelt*), now Whitehall Street, the mill on the heights next to the fort would come into full view. The gate of the fort was on the north side. Standing at the gate, new arrivals would see Broadway (the *Breede Weg*) running past the defense wall (Wall Street) all the way to the north end of Manhattan, following a Native-American trail. A Latin School and a Deacons' House for the Poor completed this small Dutch city in the New World.

The fort and the city hall housed two authorities with overlapping jurisdictions. Fort Amsterdam was the headquarters of the director (after 1647: director general) and council, the highest authority in New Netherland, which in turn was subordinate to the WIC chamber in Amsterdam (one of the five chambers that controlled the company). The director and his Amsterdam-appointed councilors were in charge of the overall government of the colony. They also acted as a criminal court and as the court of appeals for civil cases.

Replacing the previous advisory council, the city government of New Amsterdam was instituted in 1653, after a number of years of conflict between the colonists and local WIC officials. After purging

Portrait of Director General
Petrus Stuyvesant, undated, by
Susan Rivington Stuyvesant

the advisory council of colonists hostile towards the WIC, Director
General Petrus Stuyvesant (ca. 1612–1672) and his councilors felt it was
safe to propose the creation of a city government to their superiors.
The WIC directors in Amsterdam quickly agreed. Although occasionally
minor conflicts arose, the city government and the colonial
government generally collaborated amicably. The New Amsterdam
city government could regulate its own matters, such as economic
affairs (the supervision of weights and measures), public works (the
construction of bridges and roads, the appointment of a rattle watch),
and education. In 1653 the very first mayors (*burgemeesters*) of New
Amsterdam, Arent van Hattem and Martin Cregier, were appointed to
govern the town, together with the aldermen (*schepenen*). The mayors
took care of administrative matters, while the five aldermen focused
on court cases, with a sheriff (*schout*) acting as prosecutor.

 In this chapter we provide the reader with two tours. The
first comprises a walk in downtown Manhattan to explore the
traces of former New Amsterdam. We suggest starting at Wall
Street and walking roughly south towards Battery Park.

 In the days of New Netherland, long before the street grid
of Manhattan was put in place, Broadway formed the virtual
spine of the island; a tour of Lower Manhattan should be
 followed by one that continues north on Broadway. However,
to explore the Dutch heritage of the island today, you must
 follow a zig-zig route that will take you to the present-day
Lower East Side before continuing north. A longer tour of
Manhattan is possible by bicycle, public transit, or car.

Downtown Manhattan

Not a single building from the 17th century survived the city fires
of 1776 and 1835 and the subsequent development of New York's
Financial District into its present forest of high-rise buildings.
However, the original street plan of New Amsterdam is still evident.
When comparing a modern map of the southern tip of Manhattan
with old maps of New Amsterdam, the development that first
catches the eye is the extent of landfill that widened Manhattan over
four centuries on both its east and west sides. In 1609 the shoreline
along the Hudson River was at today's Greenwich Street; today's
Battery Park was under water. At that time, the southern tip of New
Amsterdam was a small cape just west of modern Whitehall Street.
On the bank of the East River, the shoreline ran along the south side
of Pearl Street—now indicated with blue lines on the pavement—up
to Wall Street, the northern edge of the settlement. New Amsterdam
was a small town—everyone lived within a few minutes walking
distance of each other.

Today your imagination has to reconstruct the old town with
the help of several commemorative plaques. While some of these
plaques date from the 19th century, others were placed in connection
with the tricentennial of Henry Hudson's 1609 voyage in 1909, which
inspired the Dutch Republic to establish its North American colony.

The southern tip of Manhattan today

The 2009 celebrations led to new historical markers at several sites. They commemorate buildings as well as New Amsterdam inhabitants, such as poet Jacob Steendam, Director General Petrus Stuyvesant, Jewish merchant Asser Levy, and tavernkeeper Andries Rees.

Some of the streets in the Financial District still bear names that indicate their Dutch background, albeit in translated form: Broadway (*Breede Weg*), Pearl Street (*Paerl Straet*), Wall Street (*Langs de Wal*), New Street (*Nieuwe Straet*), Beaver Street (*Bever Straet*), Marketfield Street (*Marckvelt Straet*), and Bridge Street (*Brug Straet*). But other streets have been renamed beyond recognition: Broad Street does not reflect the old canal of the *Heeren Gracht*, Whitehall Street bears no relation to New Amsterdam's *Beurs Straet*, Stone Street does not even sound like *Brouwers Straet*. In many ways, the story of the street names illustrates the extent to which the remnants of New Amsterdam have been Americanized.

Wall Street (*Langs de Wal*)

Wall Street at Broadway
MAP 1 › E1

Just across from Trinity Church, on the south side of the corner of Wall Street and Broadway, a small **plaque** commemorates the defensive works that gave Wall Street its name. In 1653, during the First Anglo-Dutch War, the director general and council, in close collaboration with the new city government, decided to protect the northern edge of New Amsterdam with a palisade, breastwork, and ditch. Symbolically, the palisade has been partly re-created in the Wall Street pavement with rectangular wooden blocks that delineate the possible original site. While the palisade (actually a row of posts with 12-foot-high stakes and horizontal planks) was constructed by New Amsterdam carpenters, all citizens of New Amsterdam were required to assist in digging the ditch. By the end of the 17th century, New York began to expand beyond the city's original northern edge, and whatever remained of the defensive works was removed. Today, of course, Wall Street's fame is based on finance rather than fortifications.

Broad Street

Another **plaque** is affixed to the building of the
New York Stock Exchange. It commemorates
Alexander Carolus Curtius, once master of New
Amsterdam's Latin School. Curtius' two-year
sojourn in New Amsterdam—he left to teach
at the University of Leiden—was reason for a
Lithuanian Committee to honor the man. **Broad
Street** has special paving denoting the canal
(*Heeren Gracht*) that once ran down that street.

Plaque on New York
Stock Exchange
18 Broad Street
MAP 1 › F1

Muddy Lane (*Slijcksteeg*)

From Wall Street you can easily walk down to
South William Street, formerly known as Muddy
Lane (*Slijcksteeg*) and subsequently Mill Street
because of the mill that once stood there and that
hosted both early Protestant and Jewish religious
meetings in a large room on the first floor. Later,
the first Jewish Synagogue (long gone) was
built on this street. Some of the millstones of the
windmill, dug up in the 19th century, may now
be seen in the synagogue of the **Congregation
Shearith Israel** and in the **West End Collegiate
Church. Neo-Renaissance facades** on this street
are good examples of the late-19th-century Dutch
Colonial Revival style in architecture.

Congregation
Shearith Israel
2 West 70th Street
off Central Park West
MAP 2 › E2

West End Collegiate
Church
368 West End Avenue
at 77th Street
MAP 2 › E2

Neo-Renaissance Facades
13 and 15 South William
Street
MAP X › F3

Mill stones from the Mill
Street Synagogue, ca.
1695, now at Congregation
Shearith Israel in the City
of New York

New Netherland on Old Maps

Robert Braeken

In the 17th century, maps were an essential part of the Dutch culture. They were indispensable, for instance, during the Eighty Years' War with Spain, for the reclamation of flooded terrain into *polders* (low-lying tracts of land enclosed by dikes), and for the maritime trade with overseas markets. It's no wonder that Dutch maps are important testimonials to the colonization of New Netherland—from its beginning until its end in 1674.

In 1614 a request made by Dutch traders to the States General (*Staten Generaal*), the governing body of the Dutch Republic, for exclusive rights for trading and shipping in New Netherland was accompanied by a map of the area of the proposed monopoly extending between the Delaware and Connecticut Rivers. This "*Figuratieve Caerte,*" based on local surveys by Adriaen Block, was the first map to name the area *Nieu Nederlandt* and to picture Manhattan as an island.

While these and other manuscript (hand-drawn) maps played an important role in the first phase of Dutch involvement with New Netherland, printed maps have had a much wider circulation and influence on the general public. From 1630 on, printed maps and sea charts of the area were published in Amsterdam as illustrations to chronicles and travel accounts; they were also published in Dutch atlases, such as those by the famous mapmaker Willem Blaeu. These maps were all printed from engraved copperplates. The image on a plate could be polished out and re-engraved, showing changes that occurred in an area in successive editions of a map.

Cornelis Danckerts' map of New Netherland, ca. 1665, stands out as a pictorial prospectus: it offers a picture of the colony's main settlement, New Amsterdam; an overview of its hinterland; and illustrations of the area's native population and its wildlife. The wildlife is, of course, represented by fur-bearing animals: beavers, otters, and foxes; a deer and a turkey are also pictured, promising food on the table to prospective settlers. In a later edition of the Danckerts map, animals brought to New Netherland from Europe—horses, cows, and goats—

Adriaen Block's figurative map of Chesapeake
Bay to Penobscot Bay was the first map to
include the name New Netherland

make their appearance in the landscape. This imagery vividly
illustrates the continuing encroachment of Europeans on
Indian territory.

After English forces captured New Amsterdam and New
Netherland in 1664, a new version of Danckerts' map of New
Netherland was published. It documents this event, with its view
of "Nieuw Amsterdam recently named New jorck" (the use of
the lower case "j" on those maps was possibly intended to insult a
detested English enemy).

Again, when the Dutch recaptured their former territory in
1673 but had to give it up the next year, this was illustrated on their
maps: the "Restitutio" view is described in its Dutch caption as
being of "Nieuw Amsterdam, recently named New jork, and now
re-captured by Netherlanders on August 24, 1673." "Restitutio"
here signifies reinstatement to its rightful owners. However, this
was not to last long. To establish a much-needed peace, the Dutch
ceded New Netherland to the English in 1674. This map was then
republished with an additional caption line stating: "and finally
ceded to the English again."

Map of New Netherland by C. Danckerts, c. 1665. Note the European animals in Minquaas territory, in the lower left part of this map.

Charioquet

Rio St. Laurens al.

De G

NOVA B

TRIONA

Canomakers

Canoma — kers

t' Ior

Modus muniendi apud Mahikanenses
Maniere van Woonplaetsen ofte Dorpen der Mahicans
ende andre Natien haer geburen

Armeomecks

Sennecaas

Minnessinck

t'Landt van Ba

PENN

Gacheos
Gachoy

t' Schopinaikonck

Capitanasses
Capitanasses

Matanac:
koules

Mecharienkonck

Lotteras

SYL

Muntaga

Sasquesahanough fluvius

Konekotays

Ouojuttahaga

PAR

Minquaas
Minquaas

V

Minquaas

Sasquesahanough

Sasquesaha:
nough

Yerlu

Pars

NIA

Attaock

Stadt Huys Block

Corner of Pearl Street
and Coenties Alley
MAP 1 › F3

From South William Street, Mill Lane cuts through to Stone Street, a charming cobblestone street lined with restaurants. From there you may walk southwest on South William Street toward Broad Street; turn left to reach the former Goldman Sachs headquarters. When the building was constructed in the 1980s, it divided Stone Street into two sections. The street continues as a passage through the building.

Excavations that were done ca. 1980 on Pearl Street, close to the small park of Coenties Slip (once an inlet named after a prominent New Amsterdam merchant Conraet ten Eyck, or Eijck), revealed the exact location of New Amsterdam's former city hall, even though the visible remains are actually those of the Francis Lovelace Tavern of the late 17th century. The site, known as the **Stadt Huys Block,** is now mostly occupied by the former Goldman Sachs headquarters. At its southeastern corner, colored pavement indicates the outline of the colonial buildings. A small part of their foundations may be seen through a glass panel set in the pavement.

Very few sites of New Amsterdam have been excavated in a way that satisfies scholars. Apart from the Stadt Huys Block, the only other site within the boundaries of New Amsterdam that has been properly researched is the one now occupied

by the Broad Financial Center (33 Whitehall Street
at Pearl Street), excavated in the early 1980s.
Excavations around the World Trade Center site
fell outside of New Amsterdam's boundaries.
These revealed parts of a ship, initially believed to
have been the famous *Tiger* (*Tijger*), the vessel of
explorer Adriaen Block (ca. 1567–1627), which was
destroyed by fire in 1613. Later research concluded
that the wooden remains belonged to a ship of a
later period.

Fraunces Tavern

Further east on Pearl Street, on the other side
of the street, stands **Fraunces Tavern,** a historic
site mainly associated with George Washington,
who gave a famous dinner and farewell speech
to his officers in this building at the conclusion
of the American Revolution in 1783. The actual
house, built in 1719 with yellow bricks imported
from Holland, replaced the original mansion
of Stephanus Van Cortlandt (1643–1700). His
descendants through the Delancey family had sold
the property to Samuel Fraunces, who turned the
house into a tavern.

54 Pearl Street
at Broad Street
MAP 1 › E3

First Location of the
Dutch Reformed Church

Across the street from Fraunces Tavern, a **plaque**
on an otherwise unremarkable building at the
corner of Broad Street between Pearl Street and
Bridge Street, reminds us that this was the first
location of the Dutch Reformed Church in New
Amsterdam, before a new church building was
constructed inside the fort.

100 Broad Street
Plaque on Pearl Street
MAP 1 › E3

Fort Amsterdam

1 Bowling Green
MAP 1 › D3

A **plaque** in the entry hall of the nearby former
United States Custom House, housing a branch
of the National Museum of the American Indian,
informs us that **Fort Amsterdam** once stood here
on the waterfront. The original earthen-walled fort
with four protruding corners was later reinforced
with brick walls. Within the fort the WIC had
erected offices, barracks, and a church. However,
the fort had fallen into neglect and was no match
for the invading English fleet in 1664. After the
surrender it was renamed Fort George, and it
occupied this spot until its demolition in the late
18th century.

The rotunda ceiling paintings of the United
States Custom House/National Museum of the
American Indian were painted in 1936–1937 by
Reginald Marsh and illustrate the commerce, both
by land and sea, of ancient and modern times,
including images of Henry Hudson and Adriaen
Block. The Collectors Room features paintings of
Dutch and other ports (ask if you can have a look).

Battery Park Monuments

State Street
at Battery Place
MAP 1 › D3

Battery Park, located southwest of the Custom
House and built on landfill, is the site of several
Dutch and Belgian monuments. At the entrance,
across from Bowling Green, stands a **flagpole**,
donated by the Dutch to New York City in 1926 "in
testimony of ancient and unbroken friendship."
The granite pedestal boasts a sculpted scene
representing the purchase of Manhattan by New
Netherland director Pieter Minuit (b. ca. 1594).
Closer to the current shoreline, **a large stone
monument,** presented by the provincial council of
Hainault, reminds passersby that the first colonists
(including Minuit himself) were in fact mostly
Walloons, French-speaking Protestants from the
southern area of the Low Countries (now Belgium).

During the recent construction of the subway
extension through Battery Park, archaeologists
found several artifacts of Dutch origin, although
mainly in the landfill away from the historic

waterfront. Parts of the old waterfront walls and fortifications were recently relocated, and a section of one wall has been exposed in the **South Ferry subway station for the IRT (#1) line**.

New Amsterdam Plein & Pavilion

On the occasion of the 2009 commemoration of Henry Hudson's voyage, the Dutch government gave New York City the **New Amsterdam Plein & Pavilion**, designed by architect Ben van Berkel. Shaped like the wings of a windmill, it is located at the new Peter Minuit Plaza, a major transportation hub in front of the Staten Island Ferry terminal, close to the bay that Henry Hudson explored in 1609. Nearby, a three-dimensional bronze relief of the town of New Amsterdam is mounted on a small granite rock, surrounded by explanatory texts. The relief is modeled on the "Castello Plan" drawn in 1660 by Jacques Cortelyou, surveyor-general of New Netherland. The noted Dutch cartographer and watercolorist Johannes Vingboons made a copy of the plan. The only surviving replica of his plan was discovered in 1910 in the Villa Castello near Florence, Italy.

State Street
at Whitehall Street
MAP 1 › E4

Governors Island

From Battery Park, a ferry trip to **Governors Island,** the site of the original settlement of 1624, is a must visit, if only because of its impressive views towards bustling Manhattan. Although no traces of the Dutch fort remain visible, remnants of a windmill that once stood on the island were discovered some years ago. Governors Island is now accessible in summer and hosts many cultural events. A Dutch firm, West 8, has been given the challenge of redesigning the landscape of the southern portion of this beautiful oasis in the middle of New York Harbor.

Govenors Island Ferry
MAP 1 › E5

MAP 2

North of
New Amsterdam

Manhattan and the Bronx

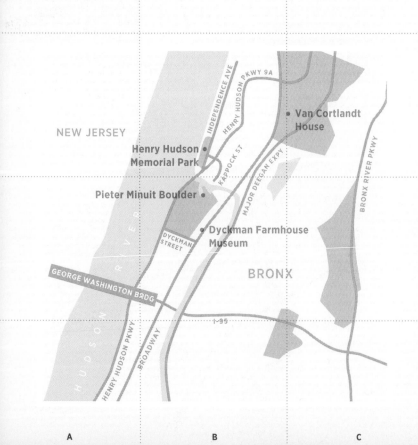

NEW JERSEY

Van Cortlandt
House

Henry Hudson
Memorial Park

Pieter Minuit Boulder

Dyckman Farmhouse
Museum

BRONX

INDEPENDENCE AVE

HENRY HUDSON PKWY 9A

KAPPOCK ST

MAJOR DEEGAN EXPY

BRONX RIVER PKWY

DYCKMAN
STREET

GEORGE WASHINGTON BRDG

I-95

HUDSON RIVER

HENRY HUDSON PKWY

BROADWAY

A   B   C

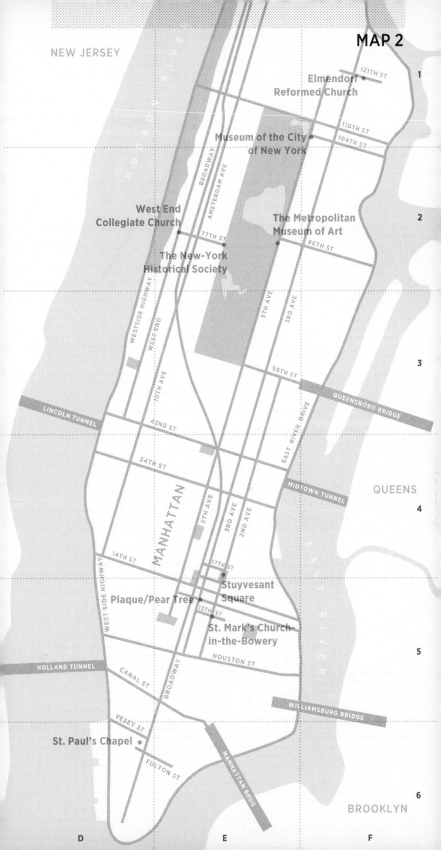

MAP 2

NEW JERSEY

1

Elmendorf •
Reformed Church

121TH ST

110TH ST
104TH ST

Museum of the City •
of New York

2

West End
Collegiate Church

The Metropolitan •
Museum of Art

86TH ST

77TH ST

The New-York
Historical Society

3

59TH ST

QUEENSBORO BRIDGE

LINCOLN TUNNEL

42ND ST

34TH ST

MIDTOWN TUNNEL

QUEENS

4

14TH ST

17TH ST

Stuyvesant
Square

Plaque/Pear Tree •

13TH ST

St. Mark's Church-
in-the-Bowery

HOUSTON ST

5

HOLLAND TUNNEL

CANAL ST

WILLIAMSBURG BRIDGE

VESEY ST

St. Paul's Chapel •

FULTON ST

6

BROOKLYN

HUDSON RIVER

BROADWAY

AMSTERDAM AVE

WESTSIDE HIGHWAY

WEST END

10TH AVE

5TH AVE

3RD AVE

EAST RIVER DRIVE

WEST SIDE HIGHWAY

MANHATTAN

5TH AVE

3RD AVE

2ND AVE

BROADWAY

MANHATTAN BRDG

EAST RIVER

D   E   F

North of New Amsterdam

Manhattan

From Wall Street, Broadway winds its way north through Manhattan, displaying its Indian-Dutch origins as it blithely ignores the grid that early 19th-century real estate interests imposed on the landscape of the hilly island. West and east of Broadway several reminders of the Dutch presence may be found, although only a few have some authenticity. Others are the result of a process of creating historical memory.

Some of the names of the streets between Wall Street and City Hall Park have undisputed Dutch origins, the prime example being Maiden Lane (*Maegdepaetje*). In the 17th century New Amsterdam's maidens used the stream flowing from here to the East River to do their laundry. Dutch Street is probably named after the Old North Dutch Church, which was built here in 1769, and Nassau Street after *stadholder*-king William III. Other names refer to individual colonists, often because they were the first European owners of the land: Dey Street after Teunis Dey, John Street after Jan Harberding, Cliff Street after Dirck Jansz Van der Clyff, William Street and Beekman Street after Willem Beeckman. Sometimes the street is named after 18th- or 19th-century descendants: Cortlandt Street, Varick Street, and, further north, Bleecker Street, Cornelia Street, and Gansevoort Street.

Cemetery of St. Paul's Chapel

209 Broadway at Fulton and Vesey Streets
MAP 2 › D6

Evidence of early settlers may also be found in the **cemetery of St. Paul's Chapel,** where, for instance, the Huguenots Jacob Le Roy (after whom Leroy Street is named) and Mary Remsen de la Montagnie are buried. Inside the chapel, a memorial commemorates Anthony Van Dam, grandson of New York's acting governor, Rip Van Dam, and the namesake of Vandam Street.

St. Mark's Church-in-the-Bowery

All of the original farms on Manhattan disappeared as the city progressed northwards, but the Dutch word for farm survives. The Bowery is named after the *bouwerij* (or farm) of Petrus Stuyvesant, which the director general purchased from the WIC in 1651. It was one of the largest tracts of land on Manhattan, running from Cooper Square north through the Bowery and Fourth Avenue to 23rd Street. The eastern boundary was between First Avenue and Avenue A. The land on which Stuyvesant built a chapel became the site for **St. Mark's Church-in-the-Bowery,** constructed at the end of the 18th century and now used for cultural as well as religious events. The **Stuyvesant family vault** under the church houses the remains of the director general and several of his descendants. His birth year on the commemorative stone is incorrect: Stuyvesant was actually born in 1611 or 1612. A marble bust outside and a stained-glass window inside the church also commemorate Stuyvesant.

131 East 10th Street
MAP 2 › E5

Pear Tree Corner

A very old pear tree once stood at the corner of Third Avenue and East 13th Street, a last reminder of Stuyvesant's onetime possessions in the area. According to tradition, the former director general had planted the tree there himself in 1667, having brought back a sapling from The Netherlands. Over the years the intersection came to be called Pear Tree Corner. The tree was killed in 1867 when two horse-drawn carriages collided and crashed into it. In 1890 the Holland Society memorialized the tree with a bronze tablet on the corner where it had stood, but in the late 1950s, when the building to which the plaque was attached was slated for demolition, the tablet was moved to Third Avenue and East 10th Street. In 2003 a new pear tree was planted on the same spot as the original tree, and two years later the **commemorative tablet** was returned to the corner,

Third Avenue and
East 13th Street
MAP 2 › E5

attached to the wall of a new apartment building whose unofficial address, imprinted on an oval plaque at the entrance way, is 203 Pear Tree Place.

Stuyvesant Square

Second Avenue between 15th and 17th Streets
MAP 2 › E4

Further north along Second Avenue, between 15th and 17th Streets, lies peaceful Stuyvesant Square, with a **bronze statue** of the director general, Petrus Stuyvesant, created in 1939 by Gertrude Vanderbilt Whitney for the Dutch Pavilion of the New York World's Fair. In 1941 the Netherland-America Foundation gave the statue to the city of New York, which placed it at this site.

West End Collegiate Church

368 West End Avenue at West 77th Street
MAP 2 › E2

In the East Village you will also find Middle Collegiate Church, one of the four Collegiate Churches that descended from the Dutch Reformed Church of New Amsterdam. The other three churches are Marble Collegiate Church (1 West 29th Street at Fifth Avenue), West End Collegiate Church (368 West End Avenue at West 77th Street), and Fort Washington Collegiate Church (729 West 181st Street between Bennett and Ft. Washington Avenues). All have plaques and memorabilia as reminders of their Dutch origins. At **West End Collegiate Church** these origins are evident in the architecture. Built in the Colonial Revival style, its step gables were modeled after a 1606 building, the meat market (*Vleeshal*) in the Dutch town of Haarlem. West End Collegiate Church also boasts stained-glass windows and plaques that commemorate its links with The Netherlands and the House of Orange.

OPPOSITE: Statue of Peter Stuyvesant (detail) by Gertrude Vanderbilt Whitney in Stuyvesant Square

Three Museums with Dutch Collections

Three museums in Manhattan hold objects dating back to the New Netherland period or, more generally, to descendants of the Dutch colonists: **The New-York Historical Society** has an important collection of Dutch colonial paintings, silverware of Dutch manufacture, and three stained-glass windows originating from the *Beverwijck* church in the early settlement that became Albany. **The Metropolitan Museum of Art** (across Central Park from the New-York Historical Society) actually has two Dutch period rooms. The mid-18th-century Verplanck Room demonstrates the extent to which Dutch families of New York City had become Anglicized. The other Dutch period room, the Little Winne House, represents a more rural Dutch colonial household from the same period. The **Museum of the City of New York** holds Dutch textiles, furniture, and other decorative arts. Its collection of silverware from the 18th century, when many silversmiths were still of Dutch descent, is particularly impressive.

The New-York
Historical Society
170 Central Park West
at 77th Street
MAP 2 › E2

The Metropolitan
Museum of Art
1000 Fifth Avenue
at 82nd Street
MAP 2 › E2

The Museum of the
City of New York
1220 Fifth Avenue between
103rd and 104th Streets
MAP 2 › E1

Silver Brandywine bowl, ca. 1730, by Simeon Soumaine

Dutch Paintings in the Metropolitan Museum of Art

Walter Liedtke

Of the many reflections of Dutch 17th-century culture in and around New York City, none is as brilliant as the collection of Dutch paintings in the Metropolitan Museum (although the Frick Collection also boasts several famous Dutch paintings from that period). Numerous works by Rembrandt (at least 20 paintings, about 15 drawings, and dozens of etchings), no less than 11 paintings by Frans Hals, 5 pictures by Johannes Vermeer, and major works by other 17th-century Dutch artists (such as Gerard ter Borch, Albert Cuyp, Gerrit Dou, Jan van Goyen, Meyndert Hobbema, Pieter de Hooch, Jacob van Ruisdael, Jan Steen, and others—altogether about a hundred masters) comprise the greatest collection of paintings from the Golden Age of the Dutch Republic outside of Europe. There are, by the way, also 19 paintings by Vincent van Gogh in the Metropolitan Museum, but these have less to do with the long-standing American interest in Dutch art than with European modernism in general.

If the settlers of New Amsterdam and the Hudson Valley had an influence on the taste for Dutch art in America, it was not as collectors but as Dutchmen later supposed to have values sympathetic to the early American way of life. Subjects such as family life, hard work, individual achievement, and nature (meaning anything from scientific study to a walk in the woods) were favored from the later 1700s onward. In the 1800s, political and social comparisons were often drawn between the Dutch Republic and the American democracy, with their analogous stories of rebellion against Spain and England, respectively. However, the most important models for the wealthy collectors of the American Gilded Age (the prosperous period between the Civil War and World War I) were actually the noble collections of England and France.

In 1871 the Metropolitan Museum's vice president, William Blodgett, bought 174 European paintings in war-

Young Woman with a Water Pitcher, ca. 1662, by Johannes Vermeer

torn Paris, about half of which were Dutch works of the 1600s
(landscapes, portraits, still lifes, marines, and so on). One year
later, he sold this collection at cost to the museum, which, until
that point, mainly possessed a founding charter and a Roman
sarcophagus. During the next few decades, the great merchants
and financiers of New York built on the broad foundation of the
"1871 Purchase" by adding paintings by great names. The first
major gift was both extraordinary and typical: museum president
Henry Marquand's gift in 1889 of 37 European pictures, including
a Rembrandt portrait; 2 by Hals; and Vermeer's *Young Woman
with a Water Pitcher,* the first of 13 paintings by the Delft artist
to go to America between 1887 and 1917. Similarly, great gifts
followed from wealthy benefactors such as Collis Huntington,

Henry Havemeyer, and Benjamin Altman. Many of these acquisitions were shown in a first-ever, large exhibition of Dutch masters held in conjunction with the 1909 celebrations of the 300th anniversary of Henry Hudson's voyage. Between 1905 and 1913 Benjamin Altman, the founder of B. Altman & Co., bought Old Masters—including six Rembrandts, Vermeer's *Maid Asleep*, and great works by Van Dyck, Velázquez, and other famous masters—expressly to leave them all to the Metropolitan Museum at his death. This pattern of gifts and bequests continued until World War II. (The only Rembrandt the Metropolitan ever purchased was *Aristotle with a Bust of Homer*, at auction in 1961). Since then, curators of Dutch art have rounded out a collection that currently numbers 228 Dutch paintings. And, like the tulips on Park Avenue, many more will appear in the years to come.

Aristotle with a Bust of Homer, 1653, by Rembrandt van Rijn

Elmendorf Reformed Church

171 East 121st Street
between Sylvan Place
and Third Avenue
MAP 2 › F1

Haarlem—or rather, *Haerlem*—was the name of
a once-small farming village, just northeast of
modern Central Park. Neither the village street
plan nor any of its 17th-century buildings have
withstood the advance of civilization.

The original location of the village center was
First Avenue just north of 125th Street. A simple
wooden church building was erected in 1665 near
the center, on the site of present-day First Avenue
between 126th Street and 127th Street, at that
time on the shoreline of the East River. In 1686 the
congregation moved southwest to larger facilities,
after which about a quarter of the original church
site was used as a cemetery (designated on a
1910 map as a "negro burying ground"). The site
is now a New York City public bus depot. The
congregation continues today in the ca. 1910
Elmendorf Reform Church.

Dutch Colonial Revival-Style Architecture

459 West 144th Street
MAP 2 › A6

Returning to Broadway, which continues north
to the tip of Manhattan, you may see evidence
of Dutch Colonial Revival-style architecture
between Broadway and Riverside Drive. The
private residence at **459 West 144th Street,**
between Convent Avenue and Amsterdam
Avenue, designed by William E. Mowbray in 1888,
represents an architect's idea of a townhouse built
by wealthy Dutch burghers in the 17th century.

Dyckman Farmhouse Museum

4881 Broadway
at 204th Street
MAP 2 › A5

In the northernmost part of Manhattan, the
Dyckman Farmhouse Museum is the oldest, and
the only remaining, farmhouse in Manhattan, built
ca. 1784 by William Dyckman, of Dutch descent.
It was turned into a museum in 1915 and restored
to its late 18th-century appearance, as was
customary in the early 20th century.

Inwood Hill Park

Finally, **Inwood Hill Park,** at the north end of
Manhattan, holds another small monument related
to the Dutch. In this wildest of Manhattan's parks
lies a large **boulder** with a commemorative text
stating that WIC director Pieter Minuit purchased
Manhattan in 1626 from Indians on this site. There
is actually little reason to believe that this was
indeed the spot, but there is no doubt that the
area was settled by Native Indians, as excavations
have proven.

184 Seaman Avenue
MAP 2 › B5

The easiest way to find this **"Shorakkopoch"
stone** (an Indian word meaning "the wading place,"
"the river's edge," or "the place between the
ridges") is by taking the A train to Inwood-207th
Street station (northwest exit). Walk two blocks
to Seaman Avenue and the entrance to the park.
Pass the flagpole and continue past the street
lamps towards the meadows/playing fields while
keeping the slope of the hills on your left. At the
bottom of the hill, turn left, and you will see the
stone at the next crossing. If time allows, venture
left into the Inwood forest with its magnificent
trees. Yes, this is still Manhattan!

Remembering the Dutch

David William Voorhees

Long after New Netherland was relinquished to the English for the second time in 1674, Dutch culture remained firmly entrenched. Indeed, the first half of the 18th century was the golden age of New York and Jersey Dutch culture. Later in the 18th century, the influx of British troops, subsequent efforts to create a national American culture at the conclusion of the American Revolution, as well as a massive migration of New Englanders into the region, resulted in the suppression of the region's Dutch identity. "Dutchness" became old-fashioned and ridiculed.

As Dutch culture disappeared, efforts began to preserve its memory. The first organized effort was the establishment of the New-York Historical Society, founded in 1804. Under its auspices, the recovery and translation of New York's Dutch records commenced. In 1835 author Washington Irving and a group of prominent New York City citizens organized the Saint Nicholas Society to preserve knowledge of the New York Dutch. Membership was restricted by invitation to those men who could prove descent from a resident of New York State before 1785—the year of Irving's birth.

More widespread efforts to preserve the region's Dutch heritage started with the creation of patriotic hereditary societies. In 1885 the Holland Society of New York (exclusively for male descendants of settlers who had arrived before 1674) was organized in New York City. (The quarterly of the Holland Society, the *Halve Maen*, is still the main publication on New Netherland studies.) It was followed in 1895 by the Society of Daughters of Holland Dames (descendants of the "Ancient and Honorable Families of New Netherland"), Huguenot Societies, and the Dutch Settlers Society of Albany in 1924. In 1909 the hereditary societies joined with civic organizations and the state to celebrate the tricentennial of Henry Hudson's

1609 exploration. This weeklong event was probably the biggest celebration ever held in the history of the city of New York.

The Netherland-America Foundation (NAF) was set up in 1921 by Franklin D. Roosevelt, Edward Bok, and others to strengthen ties between the two countries. In the post-World War II period, as a demonstration of American support for the Dutch struggle against Nazi oppression, New York hereditary societies generated a number of events to commemorate the region's Dutch heritage, such as the Albany Tulip Festival and a ticker-tape parade in New York to honor then-Princess Beatrix of The Netherlands when she attended the 350th anniversary of Henry Hudson's arrival in 1959. In the 1970s several New York and New Jersey historic sites re-emphasized their Dutch origins and resurrected such Dutch festivals as Pinkster and St. Nicholas Day. In 1971 the Holland Society organized the first of what became the Rensselaerswijck Seminars, and in 1974 it established the New Netherland Project to translate and publish the New York State Archives' 17th-century records. The Friends of the New Netherland Project was organized in 1986, changing its name in 2005 to the New Netherland Institute. In 2009 communities and historic sites along the Hudson River joined together to commemorate the 400th anniversary of Henry Hudson's explorations and the region's Dutch origins. Crown Prince Willem-Alexander and Princess Máxima of The Netherlands visited New York for a week in September of that year to join in the many celebrations of NY400. The week started with an official welcome by Secretary of State Hillary Clinton and Mayor Michael Bloomberg on the deck of the aircraft carrier *Intrepid,* including a gun salute and fleet show on the Hudson River. It included a meeting with the President and Mrs. Barack Obama, a visit to West Point and Albany, the unveiling of the Dutch pavilion in front of the Staten Island Ferry terminal at Battery Park, and a New Island Festival on Governors Island.

Since fall 2005 several Dutch-related cultural institutions in New York have celebrated "Five Dutch Days Five Boroughs," a weeklong series of events culminating in Dutch-American Heritage Day on November 16 and the famous Netherland-America Foundation's Stuyvesant Ball. A great time to visit the city!

Bronx

The area today called the Bronx was first settled in 1639 by Captain Jonas Bronck (b. 1600), who was born in the region that is now Sweden. He built a farmstead around 132nd Street and Lincoln Avenue, and a small group of Dutch, German, and Danish servants settled there with him. In 1642 a peace treaty temporarily ending a war between the Dutch and Native Americans was negotiated in Bronck's home. During the same year two other settlements were established by colonists from Rhode Island: one by Ann Hutchinson (1591–1643) near the river that was later named for her, another by John Throckmorton (1524–1580) in what is now Throgs Neck. Both settlements were eventually destroyed when hostilities with Native Americans broke out again.

Bronck's servants scattered after his death in 1643. In 1646 the patroonship Colendonck (a grant of manorial rights) was established by Adriaen van der Donck (ca. 1618–1655), the former judicial officer or sheriff (*schout*) of the patroonship Rensselaerswijck, in an area that now includes Riverdale and part of Westchester County. Also, Thomas Cornell (1814–1890), a colonist from Rhode Island, built a farm in what became Clason Point. In 1655 both settlements were destroyed during another conflict between the Dutch and Native Americans.

During English rule most inhabitants of the area were of English or Dutch descent. Anglicanism was the religion sanctioned by colonial law, but Presbyterians, Quakers, and members of the Dutch Reformed

The Henry Hudson Bridge at Spuyten Duyvil

Church were in the majority. The first black inhabitants—slaves from the West Indies—soon made up 10–11 percent of the population: in most households there were one or two slaves who worked as farmhands or housemaids. The first recorded (1698) free black in the Bronx was a cooper (barrel maker).

Native Americans left the area soon after 1700. At this time, what is today known as the Bronx comprised two towns and all or part of four huge manors. Situated entirely within the present Bronx was the town of Westchester. To the north was the town of Eastchester. To the northeast and including another part of the present Westchester County was the manor of Pelham, owned by the Pell family. To the southwest was the manor of the Morris family, which was called Morrisania. Most of the western section belonged to the manor of Fordham, settled in 1671 by John Archer (1598–1682), later owned by the Dutch Reformed Church of New York City and then absorbed by the town of Westchester in 1755.

In 1693 wealthy merchant Frederick Philipse (1626–1702) obtained from Governor Benjamin Fletcher the hereditary right to build and operate a toll bridge (the King's Bridge) across Spuyten Duyvil Creek to Manhattan, the first toll bridge in America. The origin of the creek's name is unclear. It may be a corruption of the 17th-century Dutch expression "*spijt, duivel of de dood*" ("spite, devil, or death"), but it may also originate from the Dutch verb *spuiten* (to spurt). The term "*spijt den Duyvil*," meaning "in spite of the Devil," was an invention of Washington Irving, who included it in his 1809 *A History of New York from the Beginning of the World to the End of the Dutch Dynasty, by Diedrich Knickerbocker.*

Because of its late development, there is very little to be found related to the Dutch period in The Bronx, except for Van Cortlandt Park. The Bronx also boasts a commemorative statue of Henry Hudson.

Van Cortlandt Park in the northwest Bronx can be easily reached from Manhattan by subway (No. 1 train) to the 242nd Street-Van Cortlandt Park station in Riverdale. Henry Hudson Memorial Park, located in Spuyten Duyvil south of Riverdale, can be reached by bus (via the MTA Hudson Line) to the Spuyten Duyvil Station or by car.

Van Cortlandt Park

Van Cortlandt Park is the third largest park in
New York City. The 1,146-acre park includes Van
Cortlandt Lake and features the last vestiges
of New York City's native woodlands, rock
formations created by glaciers from the last ice
age, and the site of a former Native-American
village. The land that became Van Cortlandt
Park changed hands a number of times before
it was acquired by New York City. Its first known
inhabitants, the Weckquaesgeek Indians, sold it
to the Dutch West India Company (WIC) in the
early 1600s. The WIC sold the land to Dutchman
Adriaen van der Donck, who built a farmhouse
here. Archaeological traces, probably of this
house, have been found in the lawn in front of
the Van Cortlandt House.

Bordered by Broadway on
the west side and split by
East 233rd Street
MAP 2 › C4

In 1655, after van der Donck died,
presumably in an attack by Native Americans,
many of the remaining settlers in the area fled to
Manhattan. After being ransomed out of Indian
captivity, van der Donck's widow, Mary Doughty,
remarried and upheld her claim to the property
in the name of her new husband, Hugh O'Neal.
Jacobus Van Cortlandt (1658–1739) purchased
the property that eventually became the Van
Cortlandt estate in 1699, but he and his wife spent
most of their time in New York City. Nonetheless,
the owners kept the land for farming and in the
early 1700s established a burial plot on a hill
north of the house, on the far side of the former
Parade Ground.

Van Cortlandt House

The three-story Georgian **Van Cortlandt House**
was built in 1748 at the south side of the park by
Jacobus Van Cortlandt's son, Frederick (1699–
1749). The oldest existing building in the Bronx, it
is now a National Historic Landmark. The mansion
played an important role during the American
Revolution. In 1776 Augustus Van Cortlandt (1728–
1823), Frederick's son, who had been appointed
by the British as city clerk, took the city records
out of Manhattan, fearing that they might be

Broadway at West
246th Street
MAP 2 › C4

destroyed during an evacuation. He first hid them in the mansion and later placed them in one of the family's burial vaults on Vault Hill. When the war ended, Augustus turned the records over to the new government.

During 1874, the same year the area west of the Bronx River was annexed by New York City, talks began about turning the land into a park. The city of New York finally acquired the title to the Van Cortlandt property on December 12, 1888.

The house comprises a number of attractive historic rooms, including a "Dutch chamber" created in 1918 by the Colonial Dames of New York (which runs the museum) to represent what was considered a "typical" 17th-century New Amsterdam room. This room includes a beautiful cupboard (kas) and a children's sled (*pricker-sledge*). The house also contains many heirlooms donated by descendants of the Van Cortlandts.

Henry Hudson Memorial Park

Independence Avenue
near the Hudson River
in Riverdale
MAP 2 › B4

In **Henry Hudson Memorial Park,** now enclosed by tall buildings, stands a 100-foot-tall Doric column surmounted by a bronze statue of the navigator Henry Hudson, executed by Karl H. Gruppe (1893–1982) after a plaster cast by Karl Bitter (1867–1915). Hudson faces the broad river he explored. Funds for the memorial were raised in 1909 by popular subscription in connection with the tricentennial of Hudson's discovery. The Doric pedestal for the statue was erected a few years later. The statue itself was not put into position until 1938 and was restored by the New York City Department of Parks & Recreation in 2009 for the quadricentennial of Hudson's arrival.

OPPOSITE: Statue of Henry Hudson
at Riverdale, the Bronx

The Dutch Influence on the American Kitchen

Peter G. Rose

It often comes as a surprise—to many Dutch in particular—that there still is a clear Dutch influence on American food and eating habits. Popular meals in The Netherlands nowadays often originate in countries such as Indonesia, China, Japan, France, Italy, and the United States. However, centuries ago it was the other way around, and the Dutch culinary influence reached places where Dutch sailors and traders settled, including the colony of New Netherland.

The Dutch colonists brought with them not only seeds, tree stock, cooking utensils, and recipes, but also their own social customs. For example, the birth of a child was traditionally celebrated with a special drink of *kandeel,* made of white wine, spices, and eggs, and at funerals large, saucer-size biscuits were served, as was common in the Dutch Republic at the time. These customs prevailed for more than 150 years. Recipes for those and many other favorites may be found in handwritten cookbooks that were passed down from generation to generation within the families of descendants of the Dutch settlers.

Washington Irving was the first writer to associate the doughnut, now regarded as a "uniquely American" treat, with the Dutch in America. It reputedly was brought here as the 17th-century *oliekoeck,* a deep-fried, cinnamon-flavored ball of yeast dough filled with raisins, chopped apples, and whole almonds. The recipe evolved and was simplified to use readily available ingredients. In the 18th and 19th centuries it called for 12 eggs, butter, and sugar to make a cake-like doughnut, often with brandy-soaked raisins in the middle, and became the edible symbol of the American Dutch. From that recipe most likely evolved in the 19th century the version of the doughnut we know today, made with modern baking soda and with a hole in the middle.

Pancakes, waffles, and wafers are some of the other typical foodstuffs of the early Dutch settlers. The irons used for waffles and wafers, some of them adorned with initials or fanciful decorations, were handed down in Dutch families and may still be found in museums and historic homes in the Hudson Valley.

The doughnut, a Dutch invention?

Cookies and cole slaw are two other food items associated with the Dutch. The American word "cookie" comes from the 17th-century word *koeckjen,* which in some Dutch dialects might have been pronounced "koekie," sounding like the American word. (In British English the baked good is actually called a biscuit.) Cole slaw is an Anglicized version of the Dutch word *koolsla,* or cabbage salad. There is solid historic proof of its linguistic origins in the diaries of Swedish botanist Peter Kalm, who described in 1749 how his Dutch landlady in Albany served him the dish. Slowly but surely these Dutch foods became part of the American tradition, just as the Dutch St. Nicholas ultimately transformed into Santa Claus!

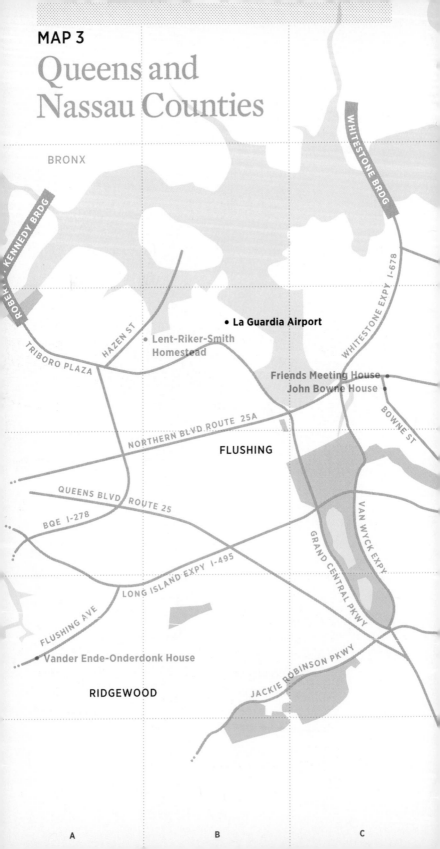

MAP 3

Queens and Nassau Counties

BRONX

WHITESTONE BRDG

ROBERT F. KENNEDY BRDG

WHITESTONE EXPY I-678

HAZEN ST

TRIBORO PLAZA

• La Guardia Airport

• Lent-Riker-Smith Homestead

Friends Meeting House •
John Bowne House •

BOWNE ST

NORTHERN BLVD ROUTE 25A

FLUSHING

QUEENS BLVD ROUTE 25

BQE I-278

VAN WYCK EXPY

GRAND CENTRAL PKWY

LONG ISLAND EXPY I-495

FLUSHING AVE

• Vander Ende-Onderdonk House

JACKIE ROBINSON PKWY

RIDGEWOOD

A

B

C

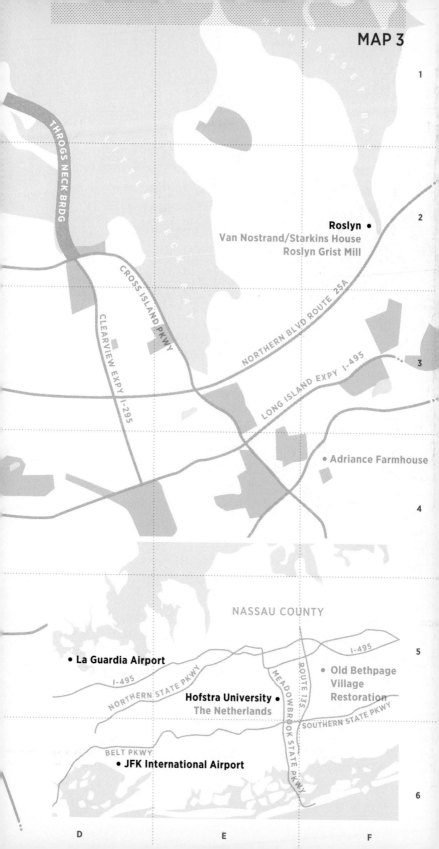

MAP 3

1

THROGS NECK BRDG

LITTLE NECK BAY

MANHASSET BAY

2

Roslyn •
Van Nostrand/Starkins House
Roslyn Grist Mill

CROSS ISLAND PKWY

CLEARVIEW EXPY I-295

NORTHERN BLVD ROUTE 25A

LONG ISLAND EXPY I-495

3

• Adriance Farmhouse

4

NASSAU COUNTY

5

• **La Guardia Airport**

I-495

NORTHERN STATE PKWY

Hofstra University •
The Netherlands

MEADOWBROOK STATE PKWY

ROUTE 135

I-495

• Old Bethpage
Village
Restoration

SOUTHERN STATE PKWY

BELT PKWY

• **JFK International Airport**

6

D   E   F

Queens and Nassau Counties

Queens is such an integral part of the metropolis that it is hard for us to think of it as rural and agricultural. But when New York was New Amsterdam, Queens was no more than a series of remote villages scattered between the Dutch western end of Long Island at Brooklyn (*Breuckelen*) and the English eastern settlements. Queens, like Brooklyn, did not become part of New York City until 1898, when both were annexed in the creation of Greater New York. Because Queens and Nassau Counties are adjacent and have a shared history, they are discussed together here.

When the Dutch began to expand their settlements, they encountered not only Native-American groups, but also English traders and settlers. From the early days, what is now Suffolk County witnessed a steady flow of New Englanders arriving from New Haven, New London, Rhode Island, and the Massachusetts Bay Colony.

As Dutch and English settlers moved closer to one another, they began to assimilate in what would later become Queens County. The Dutch colonial government of New Amsterdam exercised political and military control of this area, but permitted, even welcomed, English settlement. The Dutch chartered Hempstead (*Heemstede*) in 1644, Flushing (*Vlissingen*) in 1645, Newtown (*Middelburgh*) in 1652, and Jamaica (*Rustdorp*) in 1656. These were predominantly English towns, but they differed from the Suffolk County settlements at the eastern end of Long Island, not only in their recognition of Dutch government and their accommodation of Dutch settlers, but also in harboring many religious dissenters. Because they were not under the control of New England's repressive Puritan governments, these towns proved to be a more comfortable place for Quakers in particular.

After New Netherland was conquered by the English in 1664, the Dutch-English intermixing in Queens County continued. Some Dutch actually moved east to this area from their stronghold in Brooklyn. Both the Dutch and English languages were spoken in many towns. Also, cultural practices and traditions of both nations were evident in the architectural styles of the farmhouses and churches erected in these expanding communities, as well as in their furnishings. Even after the English language had become predominant, Dutch village

Interior of Friends Meeting House, Flushing, Queens

names continued to be used: for instance, *Rustdorp*, the Dutch name for Jamaica, appeared in deeds and other documents through the 18th century.

The Dutch and English settlements had not been without conflict. Although the Dutch Republic was well known for its toleration of other faiths, Director General Stuyvesant and his council thought that liberty of worship should not be granted to the new group of religious radicals called Quakers who had not been welcome in the New England Puritan settlement of Massachusetts Bay. Quakers had set their sights on the English settlements under Dutch rule on Long Island. When Quakers began to arrive in Flushing, the colonial government issued an ordinance that forbade anyone from entertaining them. On December 27, 1657, thirty inhabitants of the village signed what was later called the Flushing Remonstrance, objecting to this order. Although the document remained largely unknown to the general public until the early 1950s, the Flushing Remonstrance is now considered by many to be instrumental in the development of religious liberty in America and a precursor of the First Amendment to the United States Constitution. In 1657, however, the Remonstrance was not regarded favorably. Dutch colonial authorities proceeded to punish the signers. A few years later,

Quaker John Bowne was also punished for showing contempt for secular authority.

In 1683 Long Island was divided into three counties, a division that remained in effect until the incorporation in 1898 of the city of New York that absorbed Kings County (Brooklyn) and the western part of Queens. North and east of Kings County, Queens County included the largely English settlements that had been under Dutch rule. Suffolk County occupied the eastern end of the island and encompassed the towns that had been established by New England settlers. Later, Nassau County was split from the eastern part of Queens. It was named after *stadholder* William III of Nassau, Prince of Orange (also known as "Dutch William," 1650–1702, who ruled as King of England between 1689 and 1702).

Queens remained rural and agricultural through the 18th and 19th centuries. Although its Dutch identity diminished, the tolerance of diversity that had harbored Quakers and other religious sects in the Dutch colonial period continued. Today, Queens is the most diverse county in America. The population of Flushing is particularly varied. Its commercial streets are lined with Asian shops, restaurants, and places of worship of many origins—Chinese, Japanese, Korean, Indian, Pakistani, Afghan, and Indonesian. (In fact, the best Indonesian restaurants in the city are located in Flushing and Elmhurst.)

The sites described below are generally far apart from each other and, while some of the sites in Queens may be reached by public transit, a car is recommended for this tour. This tour will take you roughly from west to east through Queens and then Nassau County. Public transit does not link the different sites.

Vander Ende-Onderdonk House

1820 Flushing Avenue
in Ridgewood
MAP 3 › A5

The **Vander Ende-Onderdonk House** is the oldest Dutch-colonial stone house in New York City. It is evidence of the penetration of Dutch settlement and Dutch culture into Queens from Kings County. Its fieldstone walls, gambrel roof with flared eaves, large brick chimneys, Dutch split doors, and small windows with shutters all indicate its Dutch origins. The house was built ca. 1709 by Paulus Vander Ende, a Dutch farmer, and passed to the Onderdonk family in the early 1800s. Open

to the public as a museum, it has period rooms and archaeological exhibits and observes Dutch holidays like St. Nicholas Day. Although a fire destroyed much of the interior in 1975, the house represents the last Dutch rural household on a street that had several houses from that period as recently as the early 20th century.

Lent-Riker-Smith Homestead

In East Elmhurst stands the privately owned **Lent-Riker-Smith Homestead.** In 1654 Director General Stuyvesant gave a patent to Abraham Riker (1619–1689), and the farmhouse was built ca. 1656, with major additions by Abraham Lent ca. 1729. It is only a few years younger than the Wyckoff Farmhouse in Brooklyn. It has been well restored by its present owners and has a cemetery in the rear with 132 marked graves of the Rikers and the Lents. At this writing the cemetery is not open to the public.

78–03 19th Road near La Guardia Airport
MAP 3 › B3

John Bowne House

3701 Bowne Street
MAP 3 › C3

Further east in Flushing, not far from the restaurants and shops, you will find the **John Bowne House** built in 1661, an early reminder of the intermixture of Dutch and English cultures in the early days of settlement. Although John Bowne (1627–1695) was not among the signers of the Flushing Remonstrance, he became involved in the politics of religious freedom five years later when he permitted Quakers to worship in his home. This act incurred the wrath of the colonial authorities, who fined Bowne and then banished him to the Dutch Republic when he refused to pay the levy. Yet the directors of the Amsterdam chamber of the West India Company (WIC) did not stop him from returning to Flushing, where he eventually fathered 16 children. His Quaker neighbors were subsequently left in peace and obtained full freedom of worship after the English took over New Netherland and Quakerism had become less radical and was regarded with less suspicion.

Friends Meeting House

137–16 Northern Boulevard
MAP 3 › C3

At this writing the Bowne House is closed for an extensive restoration. Its core is built in the Dutch architectural tradition. Its principal room, a 17th-century addition, is of characteristic Dutch H-bent construction. The heavy cross-beam and corbels, or corner braces, demonstrate that Dutch craftsmen were at work on this Englishman's dwelling. Over the years English architectural details and household furnishings were added. John Bowne continued to live in Flushing until October 10, 1695, long enough to participate in the construction in 1694 of the wood-shingled **Friends Meeting House** nearby, which is still used for Quaker worship.

Double Dutch

Nicoline van der Sijs

The American English language has a surprising number of expressions featuring the term "Dutch." An analysis of these expressions gives you some idea of what the Anglo-Saxon world thought of the Dutch—alas, not too positively, even if occasionally "Dutch" may actually have stood for "Deutsch" (German). Obviously, there was not much love lost between the Dutch and the English, as the wars between the Dutch Republic and England in the 17th century attest. The English used to speak with contempt of "Dutch courage," meaning courage inspired by alcohol; "Dutch widow," meaning a prostitute; and "double Dutch" for gibberish (although nowadays the term "Double Dutch" is the name for a popular jump-rope game that employs two ropes).

The jump-rope game Double Dutch

American-English also reflected anti-Dutch prejudices. To "talk Dutch" was to talk nonsense ("that's all Dutch to me"). American attitudes toward the Dutch predilection for parsimony gave rise to such terms as "Dutch party," "Dutch supper," "Dutch treat," and such constructions as "to go Dutch" (regionally "to Dutch it")—all of them implying that each member of a party pays his own share. Rudeness was considered another characteristic of the Dutch: "to talk like a Dutch uncle" meant to say whatever was on one's mind, a "Dutch concert" or "Dutch medley" was a dispute, to give a "Dutch blessing" was to take someone to task, to have a "Dutch fit" was to fly into a rage.

Cowardice and disgrace were also readily associated with the Dutch: to take "Dutch leave" or to "do the Dutch" was to run away. (To "do the Dutch" was even used for the ultimate desertion—from life.) To "get in Dutch" meant to be in trouble. On the other hand, the Dutch could not be easily rattled: to "beat the Dutch" or to say "that beats the Dutch" was to say that something was very surprising, amazing, or extremely unlikely. However, that is of Dutch (little) comfort, all in all! The epithet "Dutch" was also applied to unpleasant matters: weeds were the "Dutch curse." The *Dictionary of American Regional English* does not reflect a more positive attitude: a "Dutch bath" is a quick one, using a minimal quantity of water; a frog is a "Dutch nightingale." Finally, a "Dutchman's anchor" was something important that one had forgotten to bring along, referring to an old joke about a Dutch captain who forgot his anchor and subsequently lost his ship. Moreover, the pejorative use of "Dutch" is not unique to the past: in 1981 the well-known commentator Walter Laqueur coined the terms "Hollanditis" and "Dutch disease" to refer to the Dutch objection to the deployment of American nuclear missiles in Western Europe.

Adriance Farmhouse

Further to the east, near Little Neck, is the **Adriance Farmhouse** at the **Queens County Farm Museum.** It was built ca. 1772 by Jacob and Catherine Adriance, descendants of early Dutch settlers in Queens. It has many original materials, including yellow-pine floorboards, hand-blown glass, and 18th-century windows and doors. Its steep roof with projecting eaves reminds us of the family's Dutch origins. It is furnished modestly, as was typical of farmhouses of the period.

73–50 Little Neck Parkway in Floral Park
MAP 3 › F4

Exterior and interior of Adriance Farmhouse, Queens

Dutch Settlement in Roslyn

Van Nostrand/Starkins House (below)
20 Main Street in Roslyn
MAP 3 › F2

Roslyn Grist Mill
1347 Old Northern Boulevard in Roslyn
MAP 3 › F2

Situated at the outer limit of Dutch settlement in what was originally Hempstead Harbor on Long Island Sound, the pretty village of Roslyn features the **Van Nostrand/Starkins House,** a small museum with period furnishings that was built ca. 1680 and has been restored to its 1810 appearance. Not far away is the **Roslyn Grist Mill,** which is awaiting restoration and is planned to be open to the public. It was erected between 1715 and 1741 on Hempstead Harbor and continued to grind grain for 200 years. Its structural framing is characteristically Dutch. On George Washington's tour of every state in the new nation, he noted a visit in 1790 to the Roslyn Grist Mill in his diary.

Old Bethpage Village Restoration

1303 Round Swamp Road, off Exit 48 of the Long Island Expressway
MAP 3 › F5

Further east in Old Bethpage, the **Minne Schenck House**, which was erected ca. 1730 in Manhasset, was moved in the 1960s to the Nassau County outdoor museum, **Old Bethpage Village Restoration.** It has several Dutch architectural characteristics: H-bent framing with a span of 32 feet, a jambless stone fireplace (no sides, just a back and a hood), and a roof with flared eaves.

Its other traditional Dutch features include split doors, round-butt shingle siding (perhaps a Long Island rather than a Dutch characteristic), a stoop, and a bed box. It is furnished with a fine collection of Dutch New York and later objects, including some fascinating old maps.

Adjacent to the Minne Schenck House is the **Carlisle Barn**, which was purchased near Carlisle, New York, and reconstructed next to the house in 1971. A typical Dutch barn, it is quite large (40 by 45 feet). The sizable dimensions of Dutch barns are attributable to their use not only as hay barns, but also as spaces for wheat harvesting. The framing timbers of the Carlisle Barn are massive: many vertical posts and horizontal struts in the barn measure 20 inches by 12 inches. Recognizable Dutch features of this barn also include the double doors in the gable ends.

Hofstra University

A previously unknown Dutch name was introduced into old Queens County in the 20th century with the establishment of **Hofstra University.** William Hofstra (1861–1932), born in Michigan to Dutch immigrant parents, made a substantial fortune in the lumber industry. After he married wealthy widow Kate Mason (his second wife), Hofstra moved to Hempstead in 1902 and operated the Hempstead Lumber Company. He and Kate purchased the 15-acre Van Wranken estate and engaged the New York architect H. Craig Severance (1879–1941) to design a mansion known as **The Netherlands,** completed in 1904, in remembrance of his Dutch ancestry. After William and Kate Hofstra's deaths (in 1932 and 1933, respectively), the bulk of their estate was committed to the creation of Hofstra University in 1935. The Netherlands remains at the center of the campus, a reminder of the area's Dutch heritage and its influence on Queens and Nassau Counties.

900 Fulton Avenue
in Hempstead
MAP 3 › E5

Holland Mania

Annette Stott

In the late 19th century the importance of colonial Dutch influences to the development of the United States became more broadly recognized than at any previous time in the country's history. Fascination with The Netherlands (popularly called Holland) reached extremes when a national magazine, *The Ladies Home Journal*, proclaimed Holland "The Mother of America." New York City's rising prominence as the nation's largest commercial and cultural center played a significant role in the emerging Holland Mania. Not only did schoolbooks teach children across the country about New Netherland, but also adult history and travel literature pointed out more general parallels in national character and historic events between Holland and America. Indeed, both countries were perceived to have started when provinces or colonies joined together to fight a foreign monarch. Both valued independence, freedom of religion, free speech, science, commerce, and the family. Nineteenth-century historians argued that the American Declaration of Independence was partly based on the Dutch Act of Abjuration from Spain and the American Constitution on the Dutch Union of Utrecht. George Washington was compared to William the Silent, and the American Revolution to the Dutch Eighty Years' War of independence against the Spanish Habsburg Empire. The Pilgrims' 12-year sojourn in Holland before sailing for America was often described as a positive Dutch influence on the English forefathers.

In recognition of the region's Dutch past, architects in New York, New Jersey, and Connecticut developed several new styles based on earlier Dutch and Flemish buildings. One of these, the Dutch Colonial Revival style, continued to develop from the 1890s through the 1940s, becoming popular throughout the United States. Interior decoration also reflected the new interest in Dutch heritage, especially in dining rooms and dens where blue and white color schemes, Delft tiles, and other Dutch objects found their place. Prominent Americans collected paintings by Dutch masters. In addition, American artists from across the country traveled to Holland to paint their own visions of "Dutchness." The majority of these paintings returned to the United States to grace the walls of middle-class and wealthy American homes. Imaginative pictures

Dutch tile from Old Richmond Town

of what New Amsterdam might have looked like appeared in fine-art and illustrated history books. Tourism to Holland increased as a result of the admiration for Dutch art and architecture and curiosity about historic Dutch-American connections, as well as fast and cheap transportation.

American manufacturers and advertisers most successfully marketed their products with Dutch images and names. Old Dutch cleanser, Old Masters cigars, Dutch Boy paints, and Van de Camp soups were just a few of the products that rose to prominence with Dutch marketing campaigns. Other companies used pictures of Dutch boys and girls in their ads or made reference to windmills and tulips. Holland Mania didn't last long, but for a few decades the national fad for Dutch things was deeply rooted in the history of New York and its surroundings.

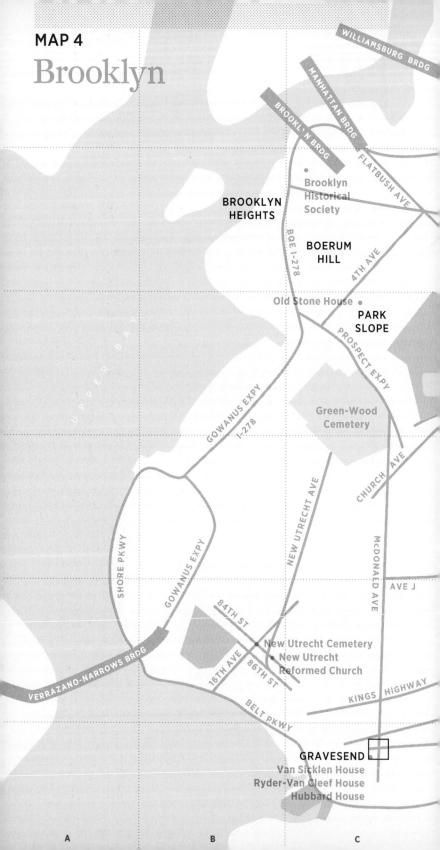

MAP 4
Brooklyn

WILLIAMSBURG BRDG

MANHATTAN BRDG

BROOKLYN BRDG

FLATBUSH AVE

• Brooklyn Historical Society

BROOKLYN HEIGHTS

BQE I-278

BOERUM HILL

4TH AVE

Old Stone House •

PARK SLOPE

PROSPECT EXPY

UPPER BAY

GOWANUS EXPY

I-278

Green-Wood Cemetery

CHURCH AVE

NEW UTRECHT AVE

SHORE PKWY

GOWANUS EXPY

McDONALD AVE

AVE J

84TH ST

16TH AVE

86TH ST

■ New Utrecht Cemetery
• New Utrecht Reformed Church

VERRAZANO-NARROWS BRDG

BELT PKWY

KINGS HIGHWAY

GRAVESEND
Van Sicklen House
Ryder-Van Cleef House
Hubbard House

A   B   C

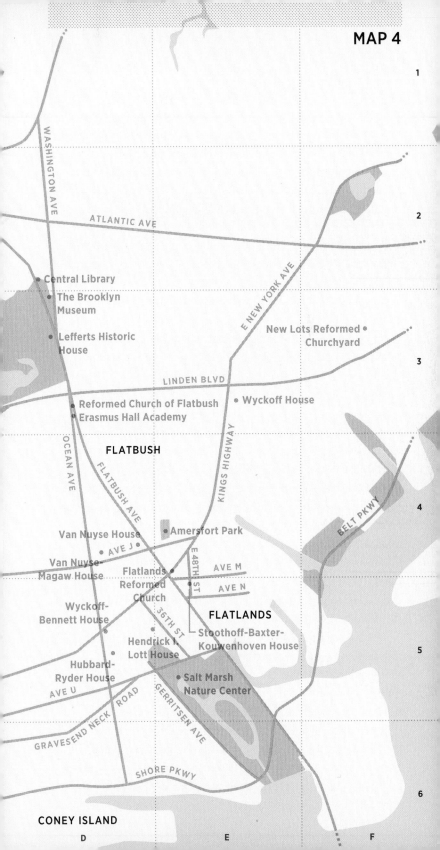

MAP 4

1

2

WASHINGTON AVE

ATLANTIC AVE

3

E NEW YORK AVE

• Central Library

• The Brooklyn
  Museum

New Lots Reformed •
Churchyard

• Lefferts Historic
  House

LINDEN BLVD

• Wyckoff House

• Reformed Church of Flatbush
• Erasmus Hall Academy

OCEAN AVE

FLATBUSH

FLATBUSH AVE

KINGS HIGHWAY

BELT PKWY

4

Van Nuyse House

• Amersfort Park

• AVE J •

E 48TH ST

AVE M

Van Nuyse-
Magaw House

Flatlands
Reformed
Church

AVE N

FLATLANDS

Wyckoff-
Bennett House

36TH ST

Stoothoff-Baxter-
Kouwenhoven House

5

Hendrick I.
Lott House

Hubbard-
Ryder House

• Salt Marsh
  Nature Center

AVE U

GERRITSEN AVE

GRAVESEND NECK ROAD

SHORE PKWY

6

CONEY ISLAND

D

E

F

Brooklyn

Brooklyn retains substantial evidence of its Dutch heritage. At least sixteen "Dutch-American" farmhouses survive, along with four colonial-era churchyards, and the borough's urban landscape contains numerous traces of its 350-year-long history as a center of Dutch-American farming. From the streets named for Dutch-descendant landowners, such as Schermerhorn, Ditmas, Lefferts, and Wyckoff, to the eccentric paths of rural routes, such as Cortelyou Road, Kings Highway, and Gravesend Neck Road, traces of the landscapes of one of America's earliest settlements are evident.

Occupying the far western end of Long Island, today's borough of Brooklyn has its origins in the six villages established here during the Dutch colonial period. Although *Breuckelen* and *Nieuw Amersfoort* were the sites of earliest European settlement in the 1630s, *Gravesande,* later Gravesend, was the first to be formally established when the Dutch West India Company (WIC) granted a group of English religious refugees, led by Anabaptist Lady Deborah Moody (1585-ca. 1659), a patent in 1645. *Breuckelen*, later Brooklyn, followed in 1646. In the 1650s *Midwout*, later Flatbush, and *Amersfoort*, later Flatlands, were chartered, and the last, New Utrecht and *Boswijck* (or Bushwick), were established in 1661. The English colonial government organized the towns into Kings County in 1683. In close proximity to Manhattan, the town of Brooklyn grew the most quickly and was incorporated as a city in 1834. By the end of the century it had annexed the remaining five towns to form the city of Brooklyn, which was itself folded into the city of New York in 1898. However, the town names, both Dutch and English and spelled in a stunning variety of ways, survive today as neighborhood, park, school, and business names.

While names may have changed, throughout the 17th and 18th centuries the population and language of Kings County remained largely Dutch as the early settlement families, such as the Kouwenhovens, Lotts, Schencks, and Wyckoffs, flourished and expanded their land holdings. Thereafter, lands were generally subdivided equally among heirs, resulting in increasingly smaller individual landholdings. This process was one incentive for sons to venture beyond Long Island—particularly across the bay to New Jersey.

The county's proximity to Manhattan was a prime engine of its agricultural wealth and productivity through the 18th and 19th

A pre-World War II photograph of the Old Stone House, Brooklyn

centuries. Ferries plying the East River and the sheltered waters of New York Harbor transported produce to Manhattan's markets and manure back to the farms. As the city of Brooklyn grew, its markets became increasingly important for the country's farmers. Designed by the prominent civic architect William B. Tubby (1858–1944), the flamboyantly gabled and pinnacled forms of the Wallabout Market complex (Flushing and Clinton Avenues in Williamsburg), constructed between 1894 and 1896, clearly referred to Dutch or Flemish market squares. Ironically, this architecture associated the marketing of produce in Brooklyn with the roots of Kings County's farmers (*boers*) just as their 250-year-long hold over agricultural production was coming to an end.

The Brooklyn Bridge, completed in 1883, provided the first direct land connection between Manhattan and Brooklyn, quickly changing the character of the town. From its zenith in 1880, Brooklyn's agricultural economy and culture experienced an extraordinary decline as farmers and farmland gave way to commuters and suburban development. There were many factors involved in this process, but mainly Brooklyn's original farmers could realize large profits by selling their land to developers rather than continuing the hard, uncertain work of farm life. By 1910 very little was left of the Dutch farming community.

The sites listed below have been arranged for a tour by private vehicle, although some are also accessible by public transit. A tour by bicycle would be possible, though more challenging. Some of the sites are private houses, some renovated and open to visitors, and others, unfortunately, are still waiting for repair. If time does not allow for an extensive tour, the must-see sites in Brooklyn are the Wyckoff Farmhouse Museum and/or the Lefferts Historic House in Prospect Park and the Jan Martense and Nicholas Schenck Houses in the Brooklyn Museum.

Dutch Collections in Brooklyn

Jan Martense Schenck House (below) and Nicholas Schenck House within the Brooklyn Museum
200 Eastern Parkway
MAP 4 › D3

Central Library
10 Grand Army Plaza,
at Flatbush Avenue
and Eastern Parkway
MAP 4 › D2

The **Jan Martense Schenck** (ca. 1675) and **Nicholas Schenck** (ca. 1830) **Houses** within the **Brooklyn Museum's** fourth floor Decorative Arts Galleries provide an excellent introduction to two centuries of Dutch-American architecture and material culture in Brooklyn. Their interpretation also represents the highest curatorial standards and a good yardstick against which to measure other sites you may visit. However, the museum's rich decorative-arts collections enable it to furnish the rooms much more elaborately than is possible in smaller house museums. Testifying to the success and assimilation of one Dutch family over three generations, both houses come from the seaside marshlands of Flatlands and were removed to the Brooklyn Museum when threatened by development and disuse in the mid-20th century.

The Brooklyn Museum and the nearby **Central Library,** located on a more elevated site, face northwest toward downtown Brooklyn and Manhattan beyond. They both hold a wealth of materials related to Dutch Brooklyn. Of particular note are the photographs of Daniel Berry Austin in the library, which capture the county's Dutch farms at the turn of the 20th century and are now accessible through the library's website.

Lefferts Historic House

The ca. 1783 **Lefferts Historic House** is located in the southeastern corner of Prospect Park. It was moved to this site in 1918 from its original location on Flatbush Avenue between Maple and Midwood Streets after being given to the city by the Lefferts family. Peter Lefferts (1753–1791), builder of the house, was an officer in the Continental Army during the American Revolution and later a delegate to the Constitutional Convention and one of the wealthiest men in Kings County. Peter's descendant, John Lefferts (1827–1893), was not only a principal of the Flatbush Water Works and the Flatbush Gas Company, but was also a director of three of the county's banks. The Lefferts House has been operated as a museum since 1920 and represents the large, finely appointed Dutch-American farmhouses that evolved in the later 18th century as Dutch families adapted elements of English Georgian architecture and decoration, such as the two-tiered gambrel roof and the central hall.

452 Flatbush Avenue, at the intersection of Flatbush and Ocean Avenues and Empire Boulevards

MAP 4 › D3

Reformed Church of Flatbush

890 Flatbush Avenue
MAP 4 › D3

Constructed in 1796, the **Reformed Church of Flatbush,** located in what is now an African-American and West Indian community, indicates the influence of English Neoclassicism with its central tower and multi-tiered steeple. At least the third church structure on this site, the current church is surrounded by a much older cemetery containing gravestones of many of the village's most notable families of Dutch descent. Some stones have inscriptions in Dutch. The church itself has some beautiful stained-glass windows with coats of arms and dedications of the Dutch families that used to worship there, as well as an old embroidered Brooklyn coat of arms depicting the official seal of the borough of Brooklyn: "*Een Draght Mackt Maght*" (old Dutch for: "In unity there is strength," often not spelled correctly in its old rendering). It was also the official seal of the Dutch Republic and of the Dutch Reformed Church. The church house across from the cemetery has some notable Tiffany windows.

The churches at Flatbush, Flatlands, and Brooklyn (now the Old First Reformed Church in Park Slope) were all established in 1654. However, the minister (*domine*) of the Flatbush church presided over churches of other villages into the mid-18th century. The Dutch Reformed Church was one of the most potent forces of cultural identity and connection with the Dutch Republic until after the American Revolution. The Dutch language only gave way to English in Kings County's churches in the late 18th century; an English afternoon service was introduced in Flatbush in 1792.

Flatbush was the political and cultural heart of Dutch Brooklyn. Its original settlement in the 1630s occurred along the Native-American trail cutting diagonally across western Long Island from Jamaica Bay to the ferry landing at the East River. Known as Ferry Road, then Flatbush Road, and finally Flatbush Avenue, this is one of the great historic thoroughfares of America. The first settlement consisted of 48 farmsteads of 50 acres, 24 on each side of the avenue. Farmhouses faced the roadway, and barns and other outbuildings extended behind them on long rectangular plots. Settlement began along the southern reaches of the avenue near the border with Flatlands, but the positioning of the church at the midpoint of the avenue's course through the township fixed its center.

Erasmus Hall Academy

Across the street from the churchyard, between Flatbush, Bedford, Church, and Snyder Avenues, was Flatbush's prime educational institution, **Erasmus Hall Academy,** built in 1787. The school was the direct successor of the first public school in New Netherland dating from 1658, as explained on a plaque next to the entrance. The Livingstons and Vanderbilts led the effort to establish it as the first chartered secondary school in the state, with cross-cultural support from prominent citizens like Aaron Burr and Alexander Hamilton, who himself had married into the prominent Dutch Schuyler family. With a rigorous classical curriculum, the academy not only provided a strong foundation for the professional advancement of Flatbush's sons, but also attracted pupils from across the region and the Anglo-Dutch West Indies. The original academy structure survives—a hidden and neglected historic gem embedded within the courtyard of the giant Erasmus Hall High School, a Collegiate Gothic-style structure begun in 1905. This public school replaced the academy and produced such famous alumni as Neil Diamond, Bernard Malamud, Beverly Sills, and Barbra Streisand.

911 Flatbush Avenue
MAP 4 › D3

Wyckoff Farmhouse Museum

5816 Clarendon Road
MAP 4 › E3

You have to leave Flatbush Avenue and head west into Flatlands in order to visit the oldest surviving structure in New York City, the **Wyckoff House,** also known as the **Pieter Claesen Wyckoff House**. This simple wood-frame farmhouse, constructed in several stages over almost two centuries starting in 1652, provides an extraordinary example of a Dutch family's growth and success in the New World. Now known as the **Wyckoff Farmhouse Museum,** it stands on its original site in Milton Fidler Park. Archaeologists discovered "oyster middens" (large piles of refuse shells), suggesting that Pieter Claesen Wyckoff (ca. 1625–ca. 1694) and his wife, Grietje van Ness (ca. 1625–1701), may well have located their primitive one-room house on a Native-American campsite in the 1650s. The surviving elements of this very early house have been designated a National Historic Landmark. Pieter and Grietje's descendants continued to live and farm here until 1901 and expanded the house as their resources allowed to accommodate changing lifestyles. Today it is restored to its ca. 1820 appearance and is furnished very simply but authentically. A key element missing from the landscape of the Wyckoff farm is its barn, which is no longer standing. The Wyckoff Farmhouse Museum plans to relocate an early 19th-century Dutch barn from a Wyckoff family farm in central New Jersey to serve as an educational center on the museum site.

Two Farmhouses in Flatbush

Joost Van Nuyse House
1128–30 East 34th Street
MAP 4 › D4

Van Nuyse-Magaw House
1041 East 22nd Street
MAP 4 › D4

As you travel down Flatbush Avenue, between Avenues I and J another small detour will bring you to two privately owned houses. The **Joost Van Nuyse House** was built in 1794. Twelve blocks to the west, you may find the **Van Nuyse-Magaw House,** dating from ca. 1800. Both farmhouses were relocated to conform to the modern street grid in the mid-20th century. Little research has been done on them, but it seems that their builders were closely related members of Flatbush's Van Nuyse family, and

What's in a Name?

Gajus Scheltema

Most early Dutch settlers used patronymics, such as Janszoon/ Jansz/Jansen (meaning son of Jan) or Gerritszoon/Gerritsz/ Gerritsen (son of Gerrit), rather than surnames, which were still relatively uncommon in the 17th century. In fact, many of the early settlers in New Netherland did not have Dutch names at all— for example, the famous Huguenot couple Rapalje-Trico, whose daughter Sara may well have been the first European child born in New Netherland, Bayard, Zabriskie, and others.

Today about 5 million Americans claim direct Dutch descent, and many of the names, whether they carry a typical Dutch *van* (Americanized as Van) in front or not, are still recognizable as such. Streets and places such as the Van Wyck Expressway, Varick Street in Lower Manhattan, and the Van Alen Institute (William Van Alen was the architect of the Chrysler building) are known to most New Yorkers. Obviously, the names do not all trace back to the early settlers, although a surprising number actually do. Well-known surnames like (Bruce) Springsteen, (Humphrey) Bogart, and (Henry and Jane) Fonda date back to 17th-century Dutch ancestors. Many became famous through later descendants, such as the Vanderbilts, Martin Van Buren, and the Roosevelts, whereas some even managed to have towns named after them, such as Voorhees and Wyckoff in New Jersey. The last two family names, Voorhees and Wyckoff, were originally place names and became later additions to patronymics.

In the 18th century a local upper class had emerged in the Hudson Valley. The Van Cortlandts, Philipses, Stuyvesants, and Van Rensselaers had become wealthy landowners, and their names still resonate with a certain pride, such as that of four-star army general Cortlandt Van Rensselaer Schuyler (1900–1993), who was a high-ranking NATO officer. Cortlandt was actually his first name, in honor of his ancestors, and its use as such indicates that traditional Dutch naming patterns were not strictly followed in later times.

Cornelius Vanderbilt, in contrast, began his career as an 11-year-old ferry boy and was snubbed by New York society for most of his life. Eventually, the Vanderbilts did become part of the "New York 400" upper class in the 19th century, along with

Street Signs in Tappan

such non-Dutch families as the Astors, Rockefellers, and Morgans. The Roosevelts became American "aristocracy" only after they entered politics, as the Kennedys did later.

  The spelling of Dutch names, which was not very consistent in the 17th century, continued to change after settlers' arrival in America. The prefix "van," for instance, became "Van," and other modifications continued to be made, although not systematically. For instance, the surname van der Beek could alternatively be spelled as Van der Beek, Van Der Beek, or Vanderbeek. In the end, some of the original Dutch names became barely recognizable to modern Dutch speakers, as they were "Anglicized" in order to keep pronunciation correct, such as Van Fleet (van Vliet), De Groat (de Groot), and Garretson (Gerritsen). Van Couwenhoven even became Conover through a slow transition process, and De Vries simply turned into De Freece!

they represent well-preserved examples of the substantial timber-frame farmhouses built across Kings County in the aftermath of the American Revolution. These houses combine Dutch and English architectural elements to form a distinct Dutch-American vernacular hybrid. One of their most characteristic features is their deep, swooping eaves, which early builders developed to help regulate heat and light levels in the harsh American climate.

Amersfort Park

Close to Flatbush Avenue on Avenue J is **Amersfort Park,** which boasts a copy of the so-called *Amersfoortse kei,* or Amersfoort rock, a relic of the Ice Age, when glaciers covered parts of The Netherlands. It was erected in the park to commemorate the Dutch origins of Flatlands.

Near Flatbush Avenue on Avenue J
MAP 4 › E4

   While Flatbush Avenue connected the social and cultural heart of Dutch Kings County with the cities of Brooklyn and Manhattan beyond, Kings Highway was the main agricultural thoroughfare linking the farms of Flatlands and Gravesend across the marshlands of Jamaica Bay. Kings Highway's winding path south from Clarendon Road is a reminder of the very different rural landscape that 20th-century landfill and

development obliterated. As the road was developed in the 17th century, it wended its way across the marshes and tidal inlets that penetrated far inland. Thankfully, the piecemeal nature of urban development allowed Kings Highway to dominate the modern grid, and this historic road continues to connect the communities of southeastern Brooklyn.

Flatlands Reformed Church

3931 Kings Highway
at East 40th Street
MAP 4 › E4

One of the most historically significant spots in all of Brooklyn is the intersection of Kings Highway and Flatbush Avenue. Here the British occupation force encamped during the summer of 1776. This was the village center of Flatlands, and the **Flatlands Reformed Church** remains, set back from the main roadway along what is now East 40th Street. The elegant Greek Revival structure, built in 1848, is the third on the site and reportedly covers the gravesites of some of the village's earliest settlers, including Pieter Claesen Wyckoff. The fascinating cemetery with many Dutch gravestones contains several later Wyckoff family graves.

Dutch Renaissance Revival-Style

1977 Flatbush Avenue
MAP 4 › E4

Just two short blocks south, at the intersection of Flatbush and Flatlands Avenues, is a charming and typical early 20th-century **Dutch Renaissance Revival-style commercial complex.** The two-story anchor building has a lively roof line of stepped gables, which are repeated on the adjacent one-story row of shops and the residential buildings across Flatbush Avenue.

Stoothoff-Baxter-Kouwenhoven House

1640 East 48th Street
in Flatlands
MAP 4 › E5

Another good example of later Dutch-American farmhouses is the **Stoothoff-Baxter-Kouwenhoven House,** a landmarked structure built in 1811 that remains a private home.

Hendrick I. Lott House

In the tidy Marine Park neighborhood stands the **Hendrick I. Lott House,** built ca. 1800. With its one-story wings, it maintains the appearance of a relatively humble Dutch farmhouse but has a large central hall and elegant Neoclassical ornamentation. Like the Lefferts, the Lotts were one of the county's wealthiest families, and this substantial Dutch-American farmhouse was at the center of a 200-acre farm. The Lott House has the distinction of being the longest continuously inhabited Dutch-American farmhouse in Brooklyn—Ella Suydam, daughter of Jennie Lott, died here in 1989. The city of New York acquired the property in 2002 and completed an extensive exterior restoration of the house in 2008. Plans are underway for the restoration of the interior and the landscape surrounding the house. At this writing, the house and grounds, which are owned by New York City's Historic House Trust, are undergoing renovation and are closed to the public.

1940 East 36th Street
MAP 4 › D5

Salt Marsh Nature Center

2071 Flatbush Avenue,
entrance on Avenue U
MAP 4 › E5

The brick, stone, and timber main building of the
Department of Parks & Recreation's **Salt Marsh
Nature Center** opened in 2000 as an operational
and interpretive anchor for the 800-acre Marine
Park. It sits at the head of Gerritsen Creek, a
freshwater stream that powered the Gerritsen
Mill from the mid-17th century until 1889. The
mill survived until 1935, and the pilings of its
dam are still visible at low tide. The Salt Marsh
Center's greatest contribution to our appreciation
of Brooklyn's Dutch heritage is its preservation
and interpretation of the natural landscape of
grassland and salt marsh. Entering through the
main door of the nature center and walking
along the Gerritsen Creek Nature Trail, the visitor
is unexpectedly confronted with a very Dutch
environment: the expansive creek that must have
made the first Dutch settlers feel very much at
home and confident that they could master a new,
but familiar, territory of land and water.

Two Private Houses

The former boundary between Flatlands and Gravesend lies roughly at Bedford Avenue. Just three blocks from here is the **Wyckoff-Bennett House** built ca. 1766. One of the most elegant and well-preserved Dutch farmhouses, it was occupied during the American Revolution by Hessian officers, two of whom etched their names in window panes. Declared a National Historic Landmark in 1976, it remains a private home, but there are plans to make it a public site. The 1834 **Elias Hubbard-Ryder House,** also a private house, testifies to the presence of another prominent Dutch family in this area, the Ryders. This farmhouse was originally located on 29th Street and was moved to its present location in 1929.

Wyckoff-Bennett House (below)
1662 East 22nd Street
MAP 4 › D5

Elias Hubbard-Ryder House
1926 East 28th Street
MAP 4 › D5

Gravesend

The center of the historic village of Gravesend (*Gravesande*) is located two miles to the southwest, where you can still make out the unusual four-square street plan of the original village established by Lady Deborah Moody and her Anabaptist followers in the mid-17th century. Its perimeter is formed by Village Road South, Village Road East, Village Road North, and Van Sicklen Street, and its crossroads by Gravesend Neck Road and McDonald Avenue, along which the F train runs today. In the southwest quadrant of the village is the colonial **Gravesend Cemetery**, visited only by appointment. (Park Rangers at the Salt Marsh Nature Center organize tours periodically).

Gravesend Neck Road at McDonald Avenue
MAP 4 › C6

Dutch Colonial-Style Farmhouses

Van Sicklen House
27 Gravesend Neck Road,
at Avenue V near Van
Sicklen Street
MAP 4 › C6

Ryder-Van Cleef House
38 Village Road North
MAP 4 › C6

Hubbard House
2138 McDonald Avenue
MAP 4 › C6

A few Dutch colonial and Dutch colonial-style farmhouses survive nearby. All of them are privately owned. The so-called **"Lady Moody"** or **Van Sicklen House,** built ca. 1730, is located directly across the street from the Gravesend Cemetery. The ca. 1840 **Ryder-Van Cleef House** was moved in 1928 from 22 Village Road North to make way for a playground that is still there. The recently landmarked **Hubbard House,** dating from 1830 or earlier, is located in the shadow of the elevated train. The Hubbard House is particularly interesting as an example of the smallest type of late Dutch-American farmhouse, only three bays wide, that was a common residence for the most modest Dutch-American farmers.

Dutch Reformed Church Cemeteries

New Lots Reformed Churchyard
630 New Lots Avenue
MAP 4 › F3

New Utrecht Cemetery
84th Street at 16th Avenue
MAP 4 › B5

New Utrecht Reformed Church
18th Avenue at 84th Street
MAP 4 › B5

Green-Wood Cemetery
1603 Greenwood Street
MAP 4 › C3

In addition to the churchyards mentioned earlier, other early Dutch Reformed Church cemeteries exist in Brooklyn. The **New Lots Reformed Churchyard** was established around 1780, 43 years before the actual adjoining church was built at Schenck Avenue. The **New Utrecht Cemetery,** farther west, was located at the original site of the **New Utrecht Reformed Church,** established in 1677, and contains grave sites dating to the mid-17th century. In 1829 the church building was relocated a short distance away to 18th Avenue and 84th Street, where it remains. Both may only be visited by appointment. The cemetery of the First Reformed Church of Brooklyn**,** which once stood on Fulton Street, as well as the Wallabout cemetery of the Lefferts family, in use between 1662 and 1849, were moved to the Cedar Dell section of **Green-Wood Cemetery** around 1865. A few Dutch-inscribed gravestones survive at lot 44602.

Old Stone House

As you turn back towards downtown Brooklyn, you should not miss one more historic building. The **Old Stone House,** formerly called the Vechte-Cortelyou House, has been reconstructed only yards away from its original location, where it stood until about 1890. The sturdy house was an important landmark during the Battle of Brooklyn in 1776, when it was attacked five times. It was built in 1699 by Claes Arentson Vechte, scion of a prosperous Brooklyn farming and trading family. The house now features a small museum, the **Old Stone House Historic Interpretive Center**.

336 3rd Street at Washington Park/J.J. Byrne Playground
MAP 4 › C3

Brooklyn Historical Society

Finally, in addition to the Brooklyn Public Library mentioned in the beginning of this chapter, the **Brooklyn Historical Society,** in Brooklyn Heights, also possesses rich art and archival collections related to Brooklyn's Dutch heritage. It is housed in an 1881 landmark building and has ongoing and special exhibitions.

128 Pierrepont Street
MAP 4 › C2

The Jan Martense Schenck House, photographed around 1900. The house is now partly reconstructed in the Brooklyn Museum of Art.

New Netherland's Architecture

Heleen Westerhuijs

Almost no Dutch townhouses, with street-oriented, stepped- or bell-gable ends, remain in former New Netherland. The buildings from that period couldn't survive the fires and subsequent modern development of New York City. Some old images of the southern tip of Manhattan, however, show us to what extent urban New Amsterdam in New Netherland once had a "Netherlandish" look and feel, even including a windmill. A few brick houses with recognizable 17th- and 18th-century Dutch features survive in upstate New York, notably around Claverack and Kinderhook, one or two in Schenectady, as well as a few in New Jersey.

As soon as the Dutch started building overseas, traditional architectural styles underwent a change (sometimes dramatic). This was partly due to the limited availability of bricks—only those shipped from the Old World as ballast were on hand at first—and skilled carpenters. In fact, the architecture of New Netherland was not a true transplant of the architecture in the Dutch Republic at the time.

However, one important aspect of typical Dutch architecture, which characterized the oldest houses in both the Dutch Republic and in New Netherland, was a structural bent-frame system with light and flexible H-bent braces. This type of frame consists of two vertical posts that are connected by a large anchor beam, reinforced by diagonal corner braces. After several decades of settlement, the population of New Netherland regarded traditional Dutch architecture as only part of their cultural heritage, since most of them had never been to Europe. In fact, New Netherland's European settlers of various backgrounds created their own cultural and architectural identity based loosely on Old World traditions. Because of the dominant influence of Dutch customs on New Netherland's buildings, the architectural style as a whole was categorized as "Dutch colonial"

OPPOSITE: The Luykas Van Alen House, south of Kinderhook, a typical brick house with wall anchors.

or "Dutch-American," although some of its elements originated in the area of present-day Belgium and France.

The "Dutch colonial" farmhouse's gently sloping gambrel roof with flaring, overhanging eaves, for instance, was inspired by the Northern French mansard roof, a style that became predominant in the southern region of The Netherlands in the 18th century. Although farmhouses in New Netherland were not exact replicas of farmhouses in the Dutch Republic during the first half of the 17th century, Dutch architectural features, in addition to the H-bent braces, are evident. These include several window types, such as "cruciform window frames" (fixed windows above and hinged casements or shutters below), *bolkozijnen* (casement windows with two vertical openings side-by-side), and "half-cross

ABOVE: Neo-Renaissance houses on
South William Street, Manhattan
LEFT: A Dutch split door at Fort Crailo

windows," or *kloosterkozijnen* (fixed leaded-glass windows above
and glassless lower sections with hinged shutters). No matter
which style, all windows were shut after dark as a defense against
the night air, which was suspected of carrying disease.

The "jambless" fireplace was another typical feature of Dutch
farmhouses. It was called "jambless" (a name invented in the 18th
century) because it had no side walls, in contrast with the English
fireplace with "jambs" or protruding sides. Consisting of nothing
more than the inside brick wall of a building with an open fire
at floor level, roofed by a single hood with chimney, this type of
fireplace radiated heat from three sides. The disadvantage of this
style was that any airflow into the house would be followed by
unhealthy waves of smoke and ash.

Dutch barn, Mount Gulian Historic Site, Beacon

Another striking Dutch architectural feature was the wall anchor, which was common in the New World as well as in the Old World. When bent in the form of numbers, the anchor often gave an indication of the year of a building's construction.

Among the most familiar Dutch architectural elements was the stoop, a platform with simple benches on each side and a flight of stairs parallel to the gable. It is said to have derived from the Netherlandish custom of sitting on benches outside the front door—often a Dutch split door. A Dutch split—or double—door, such as those in the Lefferts House and the Stoothoff-Baxter-Kouwenhoven House in Brooklyn, consists of two horizontal parts which can be opened and closed separately, like a stable door. The upper portion can be opened to let in sunlight and fresh air, while the bottom remains shut to keep children inside and animals out. The lower half, when shut, also creates a social barrier, allowing conversation with, but not entrance to, passersby.

Unlike Dutch split doors, Dutch-influenced floor plans have disappeared in most cases, as structures were changed and expanded dramatically over time. Many structures were originally built as one- or two-room homes with bed closets (*bedsteden*). As the community became wealthier and families grew, back bedrooms were often added; the Wyckoff House in Brooklyn is an example of this pattern. The most typical method of enlarging a house was the construction of a larger side addition. The original unit could then be converted into a wing, often for slaves. Upon the marriage of a son, a wing was often erected on the other side of the addition for him and his wife. It was only after the 19th century that wings were built at the same time as the main building. Very few three-unit (main section plus two wings) houses date to pre-Revolutionary times; one example is the Westervelt House in Tenafly, which began construction in the mid-18th century.

A typical feature of the Dutch floor plan which fell victim to time and changing tastes was a *voorhuis*. This interior section at the front of a house served as an entryway in which visitors could be received and from which other rooms could be accessed, often by means of stairs or a ladder to the upper floor. The *voorhuis* also often accommodated a workshop, a common practice in the Dutch Republic until the late 18th century.

Another building typical of New Netherland architecture was the steep-roofed "Dutch barn," usually clad in wooden shingles. Although not exclusively Dutch, these barns most often featured Dutch H-bent braces. Admirable examples of once-standard, Dutch barn-construction methods survive in the Hudson Valley and New Jersey.

Dutch architectural expressions also resonated in the American Holland Mania revival style of the late 19th century, as evidenced in the recently designated historic district of Fiske Terrace-Midwood Park (Flatbush) and Wallabout Market (Williamsburg) in Brooklyn, and in 13 and 15 South William Street and the West End Collegiate Church at 368 West 77th Street in Manhattan.

The Dutch architectural influence survived longest in rural areas of upstate New York and New Jersey. Use of the traditional Dutch H-bent framing, for instance, lasted well into the 19th century. In settlements closer to New York City, people soon opted to follow popular, modern English trends in architecture as they developed throughout the 18th century. Although the gambrel roof with overhanging eaves continues to be popular to this day, the original Dutch building tradition did not last. Lots of seemingly Dutch aspects of a building are therefore not original, but remind us of a once-predominant Dutch colonial vernacular tradition.

MAP 5

Staten Island

GOETHALS BRDG

NEW JERSEY

W SHORE EXPY

OUTERBRIDGE CROSSING

RICHMOND PKWY

A   B   C

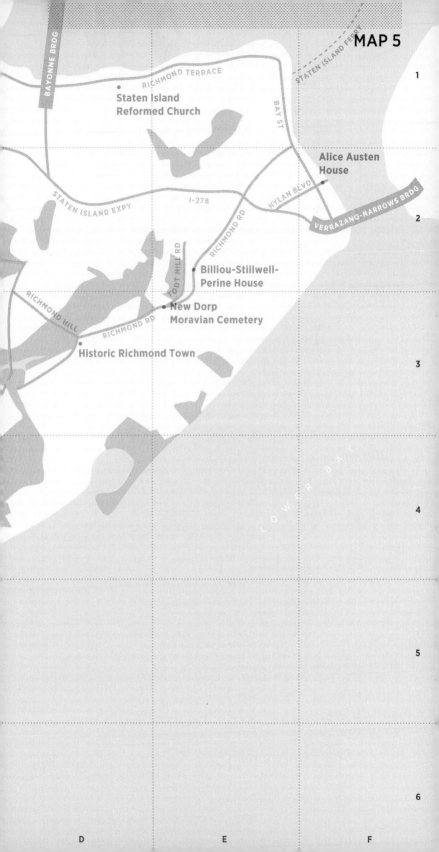

MAP 5

BAYONNE BRDG

RICHMOND TERRACE

STATEN ISLAND FERRY

1

Staten Island
Reformed Church

BAY ST

Alice Austen
House

STATEN ISLAND EXPY

I-278

RICHMOND RD

HYLAN BLVD

VERRAZANO-NARROWS BRDG

2

TODT HILL RD

RICHMOND RD

Billiou-Stillwell-
Perine House

RICHMOND HILL

RICHMOND RD

New Dorp
Moravian Cemetery

Historic Richmond Town

3

L O W E R   B A Y

4

5

6

D

E

F

Staten Island

Staten Island, named after the *Staten Generaal* (States General), the highest governing body in the Dutch Republic, is located at the confluence of the Hudson, Passaic, and Raritan Rivers near the entrance to New York Harbor. It was originally inhabited by Native Americans, and its bucolic character slowly changed only when settlers arrived. In 1679, 70 years after Henry Hudson discovered the area, Dutch traveler Jasper Danckaerts (ca. 1639–1703) traversed the island, noting creeks running deep into the country, high and steep hills, large areas of "much salt meadow or marsh," and "a good parcel of land in the middle."

From 1639 on the Dutch attempted to colonize Staten Island by means of patroonships, which were grants of manorial rights. Four of these attempts failed due to conflicts with local Native Americans. By 1659 the Dutch West India Company (WIC) had soured on the whole idea of patroonships.

On August 22, 1661, Director General Petrus Stuyvesant and the New Amsterdam Council authorized a group of 19 colonists, mostly Huguenots and Walloons, "to look up a convenient place on Staten Island and lay it out for a village." This group of colonists established the first permanent settlement on Staten Island called Old Village (*Oude Dorp*), near South Beach. It was provided with a blockhouse and a small garrison of soldiers for protection. In 1664 the settlers on Staten Island were granted limited local self-government, including civil and criminal jurisdiction.

After the English takeover, new communities were established, such as the village of New Dorp (*Nieuw Dorp*), founded in 1670, at the foot of present-day New Dorp Lane. The island's population increased gradually, and the arrival of English, Scottish, and Irish colonists and African slaves added further diversity. Stony Brook was another small early settlement that developed to accommodate the new population. Located at the junction of Amboy and Richmond Roads, it became the Richmond County seat in 1683, the year the colony of New York was divided into 10 counties. Forty years later, the county seat was moved to the nearby hamlet of Richmond Town.

The free Staten Island Ferry from Battery Park in downtown Manhattan will not only provide the fastest way to reach the island, but also the most spectacular views, as it crosses New York Harbor close to the Statue of Liberty.

From the ferry terminal at St. George, you can take buses to several of the places described below.

If you want to cover a lot of territory, a car is recommended. You can transport a vehicle on the Staten Island Ferry or take the Verrazano Bridge from Brooklyn. The route of this tour begins in Port Richmond on the north shore. From there, you can proceed to the center of the island where, along Richmond Road, you will find Historic Richmond Town. The final site is located back on the north shore, considerably to the east of Port Richmond.

Staten Island Reformed Church

By the early 18th century, Staten Island's Dutch were concentrated in and around the area that today is called Port Richmond. One of the earliest commercial and transportation hubs on Staten Island, Port Richmond was once known as Decker's Ferry because Isaac Decker, a descendant of one of the island's original settlers, operated a ferry from Staten Island to New Jersey and Manhattan from here. In 1715 the first Dutch Reformed Church on Staten Island was built here. The church, destroyed in 1780, was a wood-framed, one-story hexagonal building that featured a high six-sided steeple. The current **Staten Island Reformed Church** is the third building erected on the site. It is surrounded by a **cemetery**, called the "old burial place" in the colonial period, where several of the island's earliest Dutch settlers and their descendants are buried.

54 Port Richmond Avenue
MAP 5 › D1

Billiou-Stillwell-Perine House

1476 Richmond Road, at
Dongan Hills on the east
coast of Staten Island
MAP 5 › E2

Among the early settlers on Staten Island was
a Walloon or Huguenot, Pierre Billiou (or Bilyeu,
1625–1797/08), whose daughter Martha married
Captain Thomas Stillwell (ca. 1651–1704). The
Billiou family and the Stillwell family possessed
several tracts of land together in the late 17th
century. Their house is still known as the **Billiou-
Stillwell-Perine House.** Its oldest section may
well date from 1662, making it the only remaining
building erected under Dutch rule on the island.
You may ask the caretaker for a tour, but the
house is in poor condition and, unfortunately,
often closed.

New Dorp Moravian Cemetery

2205 Richmond Road
in New Dorp
MAP 5 › E3

Many Dutch Staten Islanders (including the
Vanderbilt family) were buried in the **New Dorp
Moravian Cemetery,** a short distance further
along Richmond Road. Behind the actual church
stands the first **New Dorp Moravian church,**
built in the 18th century in the Dutch-colonial
architectural tradition and relocated to this site.

Dutch Footprints on Staten Island

Lori Weintrob

Snug Harbor Cultural Center, a popular destination for residents and tourists on the North Shore of Staten Island, was once the 360-acre farm of Abraham van Tuyl (1681–after 1735). The van Tuyl family of Bommelerwaard, Holland, raised cattle there, which they sold in the markets of Manhattan. In 1712 Abraham, who was tax collector for the North Shore, ran afoul of the law when he "allow[ed] his negro to Cary Irone to the Smiths on the Sabbath Day." (This incident suggests the strength of the Calvinist religion and the importance of slavery three centuries ago.) Abraham married Femitye Denys, of Huguenot descent, granddaughter of the West India Company (WIC) surveyor Jacques Cortelyou. In 1755 their youngest son, Otto, launched a three-boat ferry service to Whitehall Slip in Manhattan, providing transport to "Gentlemen Travellers (sic)…horses, chaises and any other goods." This was an early forerunner of the Staten Island ferry, one of New York City's best-known attractions.

Another Staten Islander of Dutch descent, Cornelius Vanderbilt (1794–1877), modernized ferry service to Whitehall Street and was among the first to introduce steam power to this maritime transport in 1817. At New Dorp Moravian Cemetery a mausoleum designed by Richard Morris Hunt in 1885 holds the remains of Vanderbilt and his descendants. The Vanderbilt family had been affiliated with the New Dorp Moravian Church since 1715 when Cornelius' great-grandparents, Jacob van der Bilt and Nelje Denyse, moved to a Staten Island farm. Cornelius was born in 1794 in Port Richmond. He earned his first $100 when his mother Phebe Hand, of English descent, challenged him to clear an acre of the family's farmland in what is today Faber Park, in the shadow of the Bayonne Bridge along the Kill Van Kull waterway. Cornelius grew up on Bay Street and began his ferry and train service there at a spot known as "Vanderbilt's landing," near the Clifton train station, before making his fortune in railroads. Nearby, Vanderbilt Avenue commemorates his legacy.

Near Vanderbilt's birthplace is the Reformed Church of Staten Island, originally the Dutch Reformed Church of Port

Richmond, and its cemetery, which contains the graves of many
of the earliest Dutch settlers and their descendants. One of
the church's most renowned pastors was the Reverend Peter
J. Van Pelt (1778–1861). Like some of his congregants, Van Pelt
was of Dutch and Huguenot descent. When Gilbert du Motier,
the Marquis de Lafayette, also known as General Lafayette,
arrived in America in 1824, the Reverend Van Pelt was invited
to the home of New York Governor Daniel Tompkins in
Tompkinsville to greet the distinguished visitor. Van Pelt later
served as spiritual advisor to Aaron Burr after Burr's term
as vice president. Van Pelt also collaborated in building, and
ministered at, Staten Island's third Dutch Reformed Church
(now the Brighton Heights Reformed Church) in St. George.

Joseph Christopher, a cooper who was baptized at the
Dutch Reformed Church, was a descendant of one of Staten
Island's earliest Dutch families on his father's side and, on his
mother's side, one of the earliest English families. (His paternal
great-grandfather had arrived in America in 1685.) During
the American Revolution, Joseph hosted meetings of the
local Committee of Safety in his house on the edge of a swamp
in Willowbrook, near today's Willowbrook Park. In this
secluded spot the committee discussed controversial matters
that included trials of local loyalists and attitudes towards
George Washington's campaign. Christopher's house, built by
his father John (English for Hans) in the 1730s, has since been
moved to Historic Richmond Town and can be visited there.

Also at Historic Richmond Town lies the homestead
cemetery of the Van Pelt-Rezeau family. A small doll known
as "Pretty Van Pelt," available at the Richmond Town gift
shop, immortalizes one family member, a little girl nicknamed
"Pretty" who once lived in the Voorlezer's House. According
to a family story, the Van Pelts offered shelter to a drummer
named Ernst, a Hessian fighting with the Continental Army
against the British. He and little Pretty became great friends
and, when Pretty became gravely ill, he declared that if she
died he would die too. He soon was called to join his regiment
in battle. Pretty passed away in the night, and the next morning

Headstones, New Dorp Moravian
Church Cemetery, Staten Island

the young Hessian drummer was found by the roadside, shot
through the heart.

The archives at Historic Richmond Town possess many
materials and artifacts documenting the Dutch heritage of
Staten Island. Among them are family Bibles, including the 1614
Dutch van Tuyl Bible with the family genealogy. The Bibles
reveal the persistence of Dutch identity well into the 19th century,
as well as assimilation and intermarriage with Huguenot and
English families.

Similar stories of Staten Island's Dutch families range across
the island. Their family secrets are buried not only in graveyards,
but also in street names, churches, parks, waterways, and other
sites, leaving a legacy that deserves recognition. They testify to
the impact that these Dutch immigrants, and their descendants,
have made on Staten Island and, in some cases, beyond.

Historic Richmond Town

If you continue on Richmond Road, you will eventually arrive at Historic
Richmond Town, a collection of historic houses (including a small
historical museum) relocated to this area from their original sites
where they faced demolition. Richmond, the original town on this
site, was first established as a settlement at a crossroads among the
scattered farms of Staten Island.

Voorlezer's House

Until the arrival of the Reverend Cornelis
Van Santvoord in 1718, Staten Island's Dutch
inhabitants depended on ministers visiting
from Manhattan and New Jersey or on the
local *voorlezer* (lecturer), Hendrick Kroesen (or
Croesen, ca. 1665–1760), for religious services.
As the community's *voorlezer,* Kroesen also
taught school. His house, known popularly as
the **Voorlezer's House**, was built in 1695 in
what is now Historic Richmond Town. He and
his family lived on the lower ground level until
1701. As the first floor appears to have stronger
structural supports, this presumably was the
original classroom. The Voorlezer's House,
which has a strong claim to being the oldest
schoolhouse in the United States, is still on
its original site. Operated by the Staten Island
Historical Society, it is open for visitors, although
in dilapidated condition.

Arthur Kill Road at
Center Street in Historic
Richmond Town
MAP 5 › D3

Christopher House

Arthur Kill Road at
Center Street in Historic
Richmond Town
MAP 5 › D3

The **Christopher House** is an outstanding example
of a vernacular, pre-Revolutionary War farmhouse.
The fieldstone farmhouse, which measures
about twice its original 1680 size (1720 is the
construction date more often cited), became the
home of Joseph Christopher through marriage
into the Dutch Hagewout family. (The Hagewouts
had purchased the property four years after it was
built.) In later days the house was relocated here
from its original site at Willowbrook. Its jambless
fireplace (no sides, just a back and a hood) is
a typical Dutch feature, which gave way to the
English-style fireplace (recessed into the wall) in
most American homes in the 1750s.

Guyon-Lake-Tysen House

Arthur Kill Road at
Center Street in Historic
Richmond Town
MAP 5 › D3

The **Guyon-Lake-Tysen House,** a substantial
farmhouse with Dutch and Flemish influences,
was built in 1740 by Joseph Guyon on his farm
in New Dorp and later relocated to its present
site at Historic Richmond Town. It retains most
of its original interior woodwork, including both
Georgian and Federal styles of paneling.

Dutch Reformed Church

In 1769 the island's second **Dutch Reformed Church** was constructed in Richmond Town. After this building was burned down by the British during the American Revolution, a third one was built in 1808 and abandoned in 1878. Although the church no longer exists, the church's parsonage, erected in 1855, still stands close to the Voorlezer's House, at the corner of Arthur Kill Road and Clark Avenue.

Arthur Kill Road at Clark Avenue in Historic Richmond Town
MAP 5 › D3

Alice Austen House

One more Staten Island house worth visiting is the **Alice Austen House,** also called **Clear Comfort**. Its original structure was built ca. 1690: the present central parlor, along with what is now the entry hall, was the first one-room farmhouse on Staten Island. John Austen, the grandfather of famous American documentary photographer Alice Austen (1866–1952), transformed his home from a simple 18th-century Dutch farmhouse into a Victorian Gothic cottage in the mid-19th century. The large brick hearth and fireplace in the parlor date from the original construction. In the existing ceiling beams you can see the locations of the large braces that supported the original beams, removed during later renovations. Another remnant of the original 18th-century farmhouse is the Dutch split (or double) door, but Austen removed the top panels and replaced them with the present diamond glazing. Today the house is a museum dedicated to Alice Austen, who resided here most of her life.

2 Hylan Boulevard on the north shore of the island
MAP 5 › F2

Dutch culture left a lasting impression on Staten Island. Its imprint is also traceable in place names such as the Arthur (*Achter*) Kill, the Kill Van Kull, the Clove Valley, Fresh Kills, and Holland Hook, as well as more recent street names such as Decker Avenue, Haughwout Avenue (Anglicized from *Hagewout*), Post Avenue, Stuyvesant Place, Van Duzer Street, Van Name Avenue, Van Pelt Avenue, and many others.

Hudson Valley

Henry Hudson's explorations in 1609 eventually led to the settling of both sides of the Hudson Valley, roughly the area from Manhattan to Albany and Schenectady. Fort Nassau near present-day Albany was established in 1614. The settlement of fur traders that developed south of Fort Nassau eventually came to be called *Beverwijck* (literally, Beaver District). Today the area of that settlement is encompassed by the city of Albany.

Most of the early patroonships, such as Rensselaerswijck, were located in the Hudson Valley north of New Amsterdam. The valley, which was heavily Dutch in character even into the 19th century, holds numerous historic sites, house museums, and Revolutionary War forts and battlefields. Many place names of Dutch origin, such as Katsbaan, Brinckerhoff, Plattekill, Katerskill, Rosendale, Kinderhook, Amsterdam, and Rotterdam, remind us of both a distant and a more recent Dutch past. A week's sojourn in the area would allow visits to the most important of the available cultural and historic sites.

The routes described in this chapter will take you along the east side of the Hudson Valley, from New York City north to Albany and Schenectady, and then south along the western bank of the river towards New Jersey. Although a train ride from New York City to Albany offers spectacular views of the Hudson River and Valley, most sites described here are better visited by car, considering the distances between them. Also, some sites are accessible only by car.

OPPOSITE: Van Cortlandt Manor in Spring

MAP 6
Hudson Valley

Middletown ■

I-84

SCHENECTADY ◉

ALBANY ◉

■ Hudson

Kingston ■

■ Poughkeepsie

NEWBURGH ◉ ■ Beacon

■ Peekskill

WHITE PLAINS ◉

YONKERS ◉

I-287

A   B   C

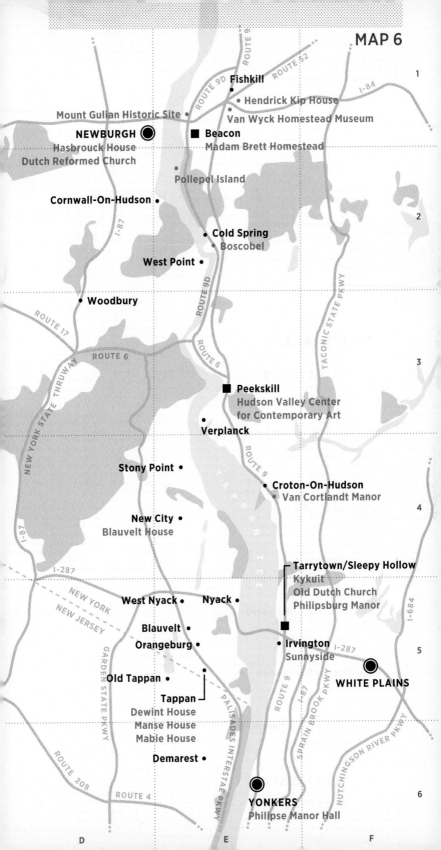

ROUTE 9
ROUTE 52
I-84

1

ROUTE 9D **Fishkill**
• Hendrick Kip House
Mount Gulian Historic Site • • Van Wyck Homestead Museum
NEWBURGH ⊚ ■ **Beacon**
Hasbrouck House   Madam Brett Homestead
Dutch Reformed Church

I-87

• Pollepel Island

2

Cornwall-On-Hudson •

ROUTE 9D

• **Cold Spring**
• Boscobel
West Point •

Woodbury •

ROUTE 17
ROUTE 6
ROUTE 6

TACONIC STATE PKWY

3

NEW YORK STATE THRUWAY

■ **Peekskill**
Hudson Valley Center
for Contemporary Art
• **Verplanck**

ROUTE 9

Stony Point •

TAPPAN ZEE

• **Croton-On-Hudson**
• Van Cortlandt Manor

4

I-87

New City •
Blauvelt House

I-287

NEW YORK
NEW JERSEY

West Nyack •   **Nyack** •

Blauvelt •

Orangeburg •

GARDEN STATE PKWY

— **Tarrytown/Sleepy Hollow**
Kykuit
Old Dutch Church
Philipsburg Manor

■

• **Irvington**
Sunnyside

I-287

I-684

⊚
WHITE PLAINS

5

Old Tappan •

Tappan —
Dewint House
Manse House
Mabie House

PALISADES INTERSTATE PKWY

ROUTE 9
I-87

SRRAIN BROOK PKWY

HUTCHINSON RIVER PKWY

Demarest •

ROUTE 208

ROUTE 4

⊚
YONKERS
Philipse Manor Hall

6

D   E   F

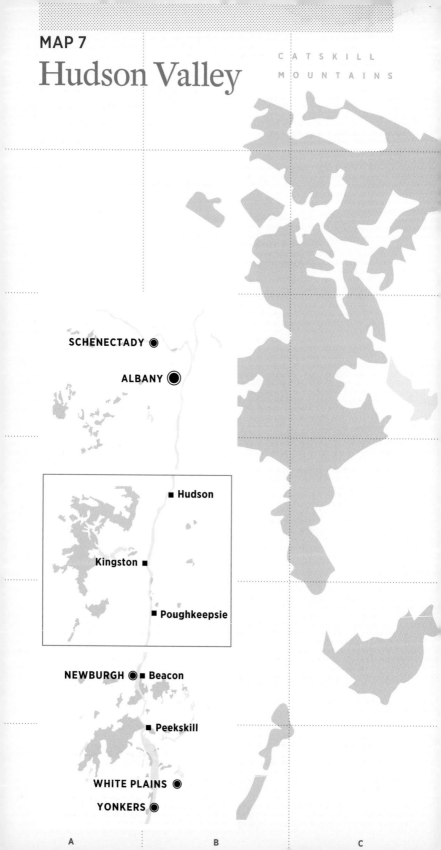

MAP 7
Hudson Valley

CATSKILL
MOUNTAINS

SCHENECTADY ◉

ALBANY ◉

■ Hudson

Kingston ■

■ Poughkeepsie

NEWBURGH ◉■ Beacon

■ Peekskill

WHITE PLAINS ◉

YONKERS ◉

A   B   C

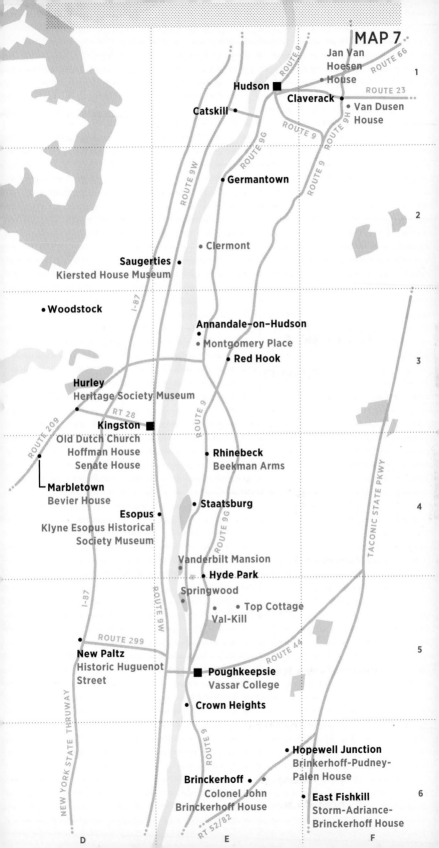

MAP 7

Jan Van Hoesen House

ROUTE 66

ROUTE 23

Hudson

Claverack

Van Dusen House

Catskill

Germantown

Clermont

Saugerties
Kiersted House Museum

Woodstock

Annandale-on-Hudson
Montgomery Place
Red Hook

Hurley
Heritage Society Museum

RT 28

Kingston
Old Dutch Church
Hoffman House
Senate House

Rhinebeck
Beekman Arms

Marbletown
Bevier House

Staatsburg

Esopus
Klyne Esopus Historical
Society Museum

Vanderbilt Mansion

Hyde Park
Springwood
Val-Kill

Top Cottage

New Paltz
Historic Huguenot
Street

ROUTE 299

Poughkeepsie
Vassar College

Crown Heights

Hopewell Junction
Brinkerhoff-Pudney-
Palen House

Brinckerhoff
Colonel John
Brinkerhoff House

RT 52/82

East Fishkill
Storm-Adriance-
Brinckerhoff House

MAP 8

Hudson Valley

• Amsterdam

I-90

Pattersonville- •
Rotterdam Junction
Mabee Farm

SCHENECTADY ◉

ALBANY ◉

C A T S K I L L

M O U N T A I N S

■ Hudson

Kingston ■

■ Poughkeepsie

NEWBURGH ◉ ■ Beacon

■ Peekskill

WHITE PLAINS ◉

YONKERS ◉

A   B   C

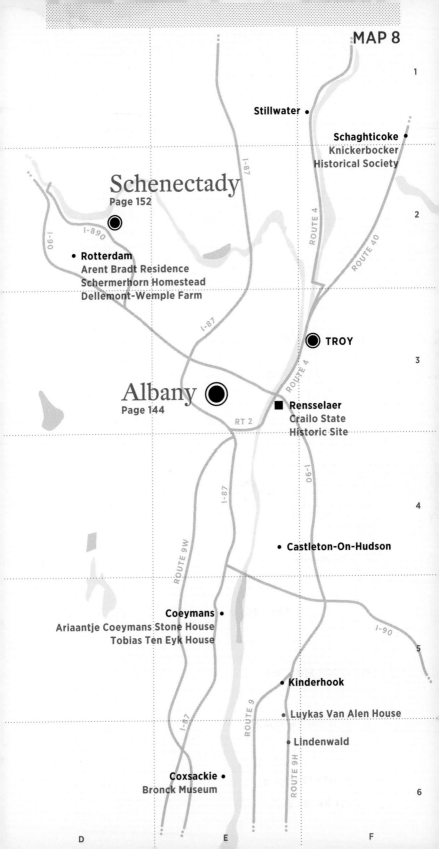

MAP 8

1

Stillwater •

Schaghticoke •
Knickerbocker
Historical Society

2

Schenectady
Page 152

• Rotterdam
Arent Bradt Residence
Schermerhorn Homestead
Dellemont-Wemple Farm

TROY

3

Albany
Page 144

■ Rensselaer
Crailo State
Historic Site

RT 2

4

• Castleton-On-Hudson

Coeymans •
Ariaantje Coeymans Stone House
Tobias Ten Eyk House

5

• Kinderhook

• Luykas Van Alen House

• Lindenwald

Coxsackie •
Bronck Museum

6

D   E   F

East of the Hudson River

Philipse Manor Hall

29 Warburton Avenue
in Yonkers
MAP 6 › E6

The Philipse family, large estate owners in the Hudson Valley who originally came from Bolsward in the north region of the Dutch Republic, mainly lived at **Philipse Manor Hall** until the American Revolution. As Loyalists, they then fled to New York City and eventually to England. The house in the center of the town is now an historic site and a museum dedicated to American history, architecture, and art. Built in the 1680s by the then-richest man in New York, Frederick Philipse, on a vast tract of land granted to him by the English crown, this house was known in the 17th century as the Lower Mills to differentiate it from the Upper Mills, Philipse's property 15 miles to the north. (He also owned everything in between, plus much more). The property was confiscated during the American Revolution, and the house served for a long time as Yonkers' city hall.

Sunnyside

9 West Sunnyside Lane
in Irvington
MAP 6 › E5

In Irvington you will find the charming home of America's first "man of letters," Washington Irving (1783–1859). Irving's fictional portrayals of Dutch country and city life include icons such as Rip van Winkle and the famous story of the headless horseman, "The Legend of Sleepy Hollow." Irving's 1809 spoof, *A History of New York from the Beginning of the World to the End of the Dutch Dynasty*, is better known as *Knickerbocker's History of New York*. Although the house is 19th century in character, its core is actually a 17th-century Dutch farmhouse. The lovely grounds, situated on the banks of the Hudson River near the Tappan Zee Bridge, are open to the public and perfectly suited for a picnic. (You'll need to bring your own.)

Philipsburg Manor

Just north of Sunnyside, at the Upper Mills, is the
other Philipse farm known as **Philipsburg Manor,**
originally dating from 1693. Here you will find
a working farm with period rooms (the "Manor
house"), a Dutch barn, and a gristmill where
knowledgeable interpreters in period dress will
demonstrate spinning, weaving, sowing, reaping,
milking, baking, boat building, and milling year-
round. There is also a nice gift shop.

381 North Broadway
near Devries Avenue
in Sleepy Hollow
MAP 6 › E5

Old Dutch Church

Also at the Upper Mills, just north of Philipsburg
Manor, is the **Sleepy Hollow Church,** the oldest
extant church in New York State, built by Frederick
Philipse. Also known as the **Old Dutch Church,** the
structure dates from 1685 and was organized by
the so-called "Itinerating Apostle of New Jersey,"
the Reverend Guiliam Bertholf (1626–1725),
who hailed from Sluis in Zeeland in the Dutch
Republic and established at least nine Dutch
Reformed churches in New York and New Jersey
between the mid-1680s and 1720. Adjacent to the
church cemetery is the **Sleepy Hollow Cemetery**.
Washington Irving's grave can be found here

540 North Broadway
in Sleepy Hollow
MAP 6 › E5

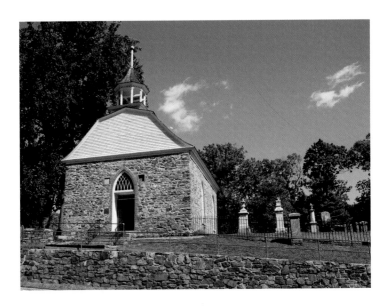

Philipsburg Manor,
Tarrytown/Sleepy Hollow

at the south end. You will also find several older gravestones inscribed in Dutch and the graves of Andrew Carnegie, Walter Chrysler, Elizabeth Arden, and Brooke and Vincent Astor, among many famous Americans.

Kykuit

Tickets: 381 North Broadway/
Route 9 in Sleepy Hollow
MAP 6 › E5

Further south in Sleepy Hollow is the well-known Rockefeller estate **Kykuit.** Although the site has a Dutch name (it means lookout or overlook, suggesting the views over the Hudson River), that is its only link to the Dutch. Built in 1906, the six-story stone house was home to John D. Rockefeller Sr. (1839–1937), the founder of Standard Oil, and to his sons and grandsons (including Governor Nelson A. Rockefeller) and their families. It has a fine art collection and lavish furnishings.

Van Cortlandt Manor

500 South Riverside Avenue
in Croton-on-Hudson
MAP 6 › E4

The Philipse family once competed for influence in the area with the Van Cortlandts, whom we have already met in the Bronx. In Croton-on-Hudson, just north of Tarrytown, is another Van Cortlandt property worth visiting. This **Van Cortlandt Manor** is an elegant, 18th-century stone manor house with an adjacent tavern and ferry site built before 1750. Guides in period dress offer demonstrations of spinning, blacksmithing, hearth cooking, and/or brick making. The house has a nice collection of furnishings from the colonial and Federal periods in their original setting, including one of the largest and best-equipped colonial kitchens in America.

Hudson Valley Center for Contemporary Art

1701 Main Street
in Peekskill
MAP 6 › E3

Keeping the village of Verplanck (named after the Dutch family which produced several Hudson Valley painters) on your left as you head north, you will arrive at the city of Peekskill. It traces its origins to the 1640s when New Amsterdam innkeeper Jan Peeck (1615–1664) made an agreement with the local Sachoes Indians, later formalized in Ryck's Patent of 1684. The Peeck family spread far and wide in the Hudson and Hackensack Valleys. Peekskill's mills, gun works, and slaughterhouses were an important supply source for the Continental Army, which made its headquarters here in 1776. Two British incursions in 1777 caused the army to relocate to the more defensible West Point on the opposite bank of the river.

The **Hudson Valley Center for Contemporary Art** has rapidly acquired a solid reputation in Peekskill and far beyond; it often hosts Dutch contemporary artists.

 From Peekskill follow scenic Route 6/202 (later 9D or Bear Mountain-Beacon Highway) to the north along the Hudson.

Boscobel

Near Cold Spring, overlooking West Point as well as the magnificent Hudson River and its highlands, is **Boscobel,** completed in 1808 for States Morris Dyckman, scion of an early Dutch family. Dyckman, a Loyalist during the American Revolution, served as a clerk for the British Army's quartermaster department in New York. For 10 years after the war, he kept the accounts of the quartermasters in London, many of whom were accused of war profiteering. In the process, he accumulated benefices and investments that enabled him to live as a gentleman farmer when he returned to New York. In the end, his lavish spending on luxuries and home furnishings cost him much of his fortune. Originally located in Montrose, about 15 miles south of the present site, the mansion was sold by the Federal government in the 1950s to make way for the new Franklin Delano Roosevelt Veterans Administration Hospital. Lila Acheson Wallace, of the *Readers Digest* fortune, donated the funds to purchase the Garrison site, and the mansion was relocated here piece by piece. Boscobel is furnished with

601 Route 9D in Garrison
MAP 6 › E2

Federal-period furnishings and decorative objects. The carriage house has an exhibition on the rescue and restoration of the house.

Madam Brett Homestead

50 Van Nydeck Avenue between Tioronda and Teller Avenues in Beacon
MAP 6 › E1

In Beacon you will find the **Madam Brett Homestead,** where seven generations of the Dutch-American Rombouts-Brett family lived from 1709 to 1954, starting with Roger and Catherine Brett. Today the house is a museum: the rooms display original furnishings and a collection of China-trade porcelain. Revolutionary War leaders such as George Washington, the Marquis de Lafayette, and Baron Von Steuben are said to have been guests in the house.

Mount Gulian Historic Site

145 Sterling Street in Beacon
MAP 6 › E1

In Beacon you can also explore the **Mount Gulian Historic Site.** At its center is a reconstructed 18th-century homestead built as a summer residence by Gulian Verplanck (1751–1799), a speaker of the New York State Assembly and president of the Bank of New York in the late 18th century. The site also includes an 18th-century Dutch barn, a nicely restored garden, and 44 acres overlooking the Hudson. Its museum is dedicated to local history and the American Revolution.

The Knickerbocker Story

Elizabeth Bradley

It took an imaginary Dutchman to reintroduce New Yorkers
to their Dutch roots. In 1809 the young writer Washington
Irving published a good-natured satire entitled *A History of
New York*. The book was the young Irving's first solo literary
venture, and it was a charming and loquacious (if not altogether
accurate) account of the Dutch settlement of the city of New
Amsterdam 200 years before. The book was ostensibly written
by one Diedrich Knickerbocker, a fictional character who
served as Irving's narrator and alter ego. Knickerbocker is a self-
declared New Yorker of Dutch descent (he claims to be related
to the actual Knickerbocker family of Rensselaer County)
and a fierce champion of his ancestors, the first settlers of New
Amsterdam. He bewails the fact that the Dutch contribution to
the development of Manhattan has been so completely forgotten
in the two centuries that intervened since Henry Hudson's
discovery of the island, and he sets about to repair this injury
through his valedictory account of the Dutch settlement. To this
end, Knickerbocker describes New Amsterdam as a veritable
Eden, populated by peaceable, pipe-smoking burghers and their
contented cows, whose perambulations, the historian insists,
carved out the crooked streets of Lower Manhattan. He provides
clever, if inaccurate, Dutch etymologies for curious New York
place names, such as "Kip's Bay," and introduces New Yorkers
to hospitable "Dutch rituals and recipes" (such as the doughnut,
or *oliekoeck*). While Irving had originally intended his book as
a spoofing rejoinder to the work of the brand-new New-York
Historical Society, the book soon took on a life and an authority
of its own. The young author's rollicking tales of New Amsterdam
offered New Yorkers a satisfying "creation story" of sorts and
also gave them a tremendously appealing set of ancestors—the
previously all-but-forgotten Dutch.

   For these reasons the fictional historian who presented this
rosy (if often ridiculous) glimpse into the city's past was almost
immediately adopted by New Yorkers as their first mascot. In
fact, the social, political, demographic, philosophical, and
architectural transformations variously undergone by New
York in the 200 years since Irving wrote may all be mapped

Illustration by Frances Brundage of *The legend of Sleepy Hollow: found among the papers of the late Diedrich Knickerbocker,* by Washington Irving.

across the competing incarnations of "Knickerbocker." The Knickerbocker identity was applied to native New Yorkers of Irish descent in the 1840s, to members of New York's "high society" in the Gilded Age, and to New Deal Democrats in the 1930s. The Knickerbocker's image (a little man in stereotypical colonial Dutch costume) was used to promote the consolidation of the five boroughs in 1898 and to sell a popular beer in the 1950s. His surname was used over the course of two centuries by bakeries, steamboat companies, spice merchants, chocolate factories, and the New York Knickerbockers—or "Knicks"—basketball team at Madison Square Garden, just to cite a few namesakes.

The name "Knickerbocker" still hovers at the edges of everyday life, all over New York City. Contemporary New Yorkers may be found on Knickerbocker Avenue in Bushwick, in the garden of Knickerbocker Village on Cherry Street, at the Knickerbocker Club on Fifth Avenue, or while listening to jazz on University Place at the Knickerbocker Grill. Some notable New Yorkers are even called "Knickerbockers." And for good reason: the chief message of Irving's Dutch historian is still the very idea of New York. The questions of urban history, preservation, tolerance, and city identity that preoccupied Irving's historian are just as lively and pertinent 200 years later as they were at his creation.

Pollepel Island

In the Hudson River, just south of Beacon, lies **Pollepel Island** ("pollepel" means ladle or wooden spoon); its romantic Bannerman Castle, originally a 19th-century ammunition storage facility, is now unfortunately in decay.

In the Hudson River, just south of Beacon
MAP 6 › E2

Fishkill

The story of Fishkill and surroundings began in 1683 when two merchants from New York City, Francis (or Frans) Rombouts, father of Catherine Brett of the Madam Brett Homestead) and Galeyn Verplanck, purchased 85,000 acres from the Wappinger Indians. (Stephanus Van Cortlandt later bought part of their share). The first Reformed Protestant Dutch Church in Fishkill, no longer extant, was built around 1731 by Dutch settlers. In that year a minister (*domine*) arrived from the Dutch Republic to serve in both Fishkill and Poughkeepsie. The current church, dating from the 19th century, is surrounded by a number of Dutch-inscribed gravestones.

Van Wyck Homestead Museum

In 1732 Cornelius Van Wyck (1694–1761) purchased 959 acres from Catherine Brett-Rombouts and built a three-room house just south of Fishkill, the present east wing of the **Van Wyck Homestead Museum.** Listed on the National Register of Historic Places, the house was visited by many notables during the American Revolution, including George Washington, Baron Von Steuben, and the Marquis de Lafayette. It is also said to be the setting for James Fenimore Cooper's novel *The Spy.*

504 Route 9 at
Interstate 84 in Fishkill
MAP 6 › E1

Brinkerhoff-Pudney-Palen House

68 North Kensington Drive
in Hopewell Junction
MAP 7 › E6

Dating back to the 18th century, the **Brinkerhoff-Pudney-Palen House,** home of the **East Fishkill Historical Society,** was built by the Brinkerhoff family after they arrived from Flushing, Long Island. It too was on land purchased from Madam Brett. The original structure consisted of a kitchen with a large fireplace and oven, a steep staircase to the single room upstairs, a Dutch split door, and an enclosed porch.

Houses of Dutch Origin

Hendrick Kip House
Southwest of Route 52 in
Glenham-Fishkill
MAP 6 › E1

Colonel John
Brinckerhoff House
Lomala Road, off Route
82 in Fishkill, east of the
village of Brinckerhoff
MAP 7 › E6

Storm-Adriance-
Brinckerhoff House
Beekman Road/Route 9
in East Fishkill
MAP 7 › F6

There are several private houses of Dutch origin in the area, including the 1753 **Hendrick Kip House,** the 1738 **Colonel John Brinckerhoff House** (an **historical marker** is located on Route 82) and the **Storm-Adriance-Brinckerhoff House,** a portion of which dates from the mid-18th century.

Frances Lehman Loeb Art Center

The next stop is Poughkeepsie and the **Magoon Collection of Vassar College/Frances Lehman Loeb Art Center,** which has extensive holdings of 19th-century Hudson River School paintings and works by European masters and 20th-century American painters. Originally settled by a Dutchman named Barent Balthus and his son Baltus Barent Van Kleeck (1677–1756), Poughkeepsie has little to remember its Dutch past. Even Dutchess County, where it is located, is apparently not named after the Dutch, as one would expect, but after Mary of Modena, Duchess of York, the second wife of James, Duke of York, who later succeeded his older brother to become King James II of England.

124 Raymond Avenue at Vassar Lake Drive in Poughkeepsie
MAP 7 › E5

The Roosevelt Estates

However, in nearby Hyde Park are **Springwood,** the home of Dutch-descendant United States president Franklin Delano Roosevelt (1882–1945); his presidential library and museum; and a new educational center, all on the banks of the Hudson River. Nearby you will find **Val-Kill,** the secluded retreat of Eleanor Roosevelt (1884–1962), Franklin Roosevelt's distant cousin and wife. The decor of both houses is exactly as their owners left it. Roosevelt's library, the first American presidential library, is built of Hudson Valley fieldstone in the Dutch colonial style and houses all of Roosevelt's papers and books, as well as much memorabilia. Eleanor Roosevelt's archive is located in a wing added in 1972. Roosevelt also built **Top Cottage** at the eastern end of his estate, an example of Dutch Colonial Revival architecture. His interest in preserving the old Dutch colonial styles was evident and led to several rescues as well as reconstructions of buildings in the area, such as the Rhinebeck post office. He wrote, "The genesis of my interest in Dutch Houses of the Hudson Valley before 1776 lies in the destruction of a delightful old house in Dutchess County . . . when I was a small boy; for, many years later, in searching vainly for some photograph or drawing of that

Springwood
4097 Albany Post Road near Estates Lane in Hyde Park
MAP 7 › E5

Val-Kill (below)
Route 9G near Park Avenue in Hyde Park
MAP 7 › E5

Top Cottage
15 Valkill Drive in Hyde Park
MAP 7 › E5

house I came to realize that such dwellings of the
colonial period in New York as had stood until the
twentieth century were fast disappearing before
the march of modern civilization."

Vanderbilt Mansion

81 Vanderbilt Park Road
in Hyde Park

MAP 7 › E4

Also in Hyde Park you may visit the Frederick
W. and Louise **Vanderbilt Mansion,** a National
Historic Site. The fabulously wealthy Frederick
William Vanderbilt (1856–1938) built the house
and gardens in the 1890s as a country retreat. He
was a grandson of well-known railroad tycoon
Cornelius Vanderbilt (1794–1877).

Rhinebeck

Following the Albany Post Road to the north, head to Rhinebeck, which
was settled in the late 17th century by Jacob and Hendrick Kip, two
Dutchmen from Kingston, New York.

Beekman Arms

In the early 1700s Willem Traphagen (1654–1732) established a travelers' guest house named Traphagen Inn, which was moved by his son Arent in 1766 to the town's crossroads. Judge Henry Beekman (b. 1651) was then, among several prominent English Crown land-patent holders, expanding his estate. Colonel Henry Beekman Jr. (d. 1716) promoted the region even more, dominating the little village where refugees from Germany's Palatine-Rhine region settled. After its move to the intersection of the village, the Traphagen Inn was renamed the **Beekman Arms.** The inn's owners claim that it is the oldest continuously operating guest house in the United States.

Rhinebeck's post office next door was built at the urging of President Roosevelt and modeled after Kipsbergen, an 18th-century Rhinebeck home that had belonged to his ancestors, the Beekmans, and that had burned down in the early 20th century.

Beekman Arms
6387 Mill Street
in Rhinebeck
MAP 7 › E4

Post Office
6383 Mill Street
in Rhinebeck
MAP 7 › E4

Red Hook

Approximately five miles to the north of Rhinebeck is Red Hook, which was first settled by Dutch families in the late 1600s. The name derives from *Roode Hoeck,* or red peninsula, possibly referring to the rich palette of red foliage shades in the fall.

Two Livingston Estates

The Livingstons were among the most prominent families in the Hudson Valley. Robert Livingston (1718–1775), a Dutchman of Scottish descent who spoke both Dutch and English, made himself useful to the royal governors of New York. He was granted 600,000 acres of land in today's Dutchess and Columbia Counties, making him one of their biggest landowners. Robert "married Dutch," as the saying goes, in choosing Alida Schuyler Van Rensselaer (1656–1727) as his bride. Significant house museums associated

Montgomery Place
8 Davis Way in
Annandale-on-Hudson
MAP 7 › E3

**Clermont State
Historic Site**
One Clermont Avenue in
Germantown
MAP 7 › E2

with the Livingston family and their huge manor on the Hudson River include **Montgomery Place,** privately owned at the time of this writing, and **Clermont State Historic Site.** The 485-acre Clermont estate is preserved as it was in the early 20th century.

Dutch Brick Houses

Jan Van Hoesen House (below)
40 Route 66/Union Turnpike in Hudson
MAP 7 › F1

Van Dusen House
County Road 29/Spook Rock Road in Claverack
MAP 7 › F1

One of the few remaining Dutch brick houses in the region is the privately owned **Jan Van Hoesen House,** located in the midst of an uninspiring trailer camp called "Dutch Village." This important early-18th-century house was built by seafarer and farmer Jan Van Hoesen (d. 1703), whose initials (including a "T" for Tanneke, his wife, who bore him 11 children) are still visible in the east gable. Unfortunately, the house is in very poor condition, and efforts to preserve it have not yet been successful. Another privately owned farmhouse, built of brick, stone, and wood, is located to the south along Claverack Creek. It is called the **Van Dusen House** after the family that once owned the lands and whose gravestones are still visible in a cornfield across the road.

Dutch Immigrants after the 17th Century

Hans Krabbendam

In the 18th and 19th centuries, emigration from the Dutch Republic to the United States stands out more for being relatively late and little rather than for its spectacular numbers. Whereas the Irish led the pack with over 200,000 immigrants in the 1830s, followed by 150,000 Germans and other Europeans, The Netherlands contributed only 1,412 *landverhuizers*. In the 1840s the numbers from Europe swelled from half a million to 1.6 million immigrants, of which the Dutch had a share of only 8,000.

In the late 1840s the number of Dutch immigrants to the United States increased significantly for several reasons. The Dutch suffered from general European economic and political crises, aggravated by the potato blight of 1845–1847, as well as from a religious conflict caused by a split in the established Protestant church. Such factors moved a group of religious dissenters to take the lead in the emigration movement between 1831 and 1880. While these "Seceders" were outnumbered by other religious groups, they left a lasting imprint on the Dutch-American community. Since most of them came from rural areas and wanted to own farms, they settled in the Midwest—in rural areas of Michigan, Iowa, Wisconsin, and Illinois. After 1880, when the best lands were taken, others moved to urban centers such as Grand Rapids, Chicago, and Detroit. Between 1840 and 1940 a quarter of a million Dutch men and women made the move to America. The descendants of the colonial Dutch from the New Netherland era generously helped these new immigrants.

Circumstances in The Netherlands often allowed prospective emigrants to make calculated decisions. Since land was the strongest incentive, most emigrants moved in family units. Their deep religious convictions spurred a separate educational system, a national ecclesiastical network, and the preservation of the Dutch language. Aided by 50 ethnic periodicals, correspondence with the old country, concentration in a few states, and strong institutions, the 19th-century Dutch succeeded in retaining their

The *S.S. Rotterdam* of the Holland-America Line

cohesion in America for over a century. For almost a century,
between 1873 and 1960, the Holland America Line maintained
a direct connection between Rotterdam and New York, which
eased the stress of the emigration experience. Even though New
York was the port of entry for 90 percent of Dutch immigrants,
relatively few settled in New York City. Exceptions included the
Jewish Dutch, who played a key role in founding synagogues and
schools in New York after 1830. Most of the Dutch Jews who came
to America were shopkeepers and traders, joined by workers in the
clothing, tobacco, and diamond industries in the 1870s. They often
remained committed to the old traditions, while quickly adopting
the English language. Another large group of Dutch (Protestants)
settled in New Jersey to work in the silk industry in Paterson.

Between 1947 and 1963, another 75,000 Dutch citizens moved
to America. Some joined the settlements in the Midwest, but a
large group of expatriates who left Indonesia after the country
gained independence from The Netherlands in the late 1940s found
jobs in the service sector, mainly in California. After that period,
Dutch emigration to the United States decreased significantly
because of the post-war economic boom in The Netherlands.
However, a steady stream of Dutch professionals, artists, and a
few farmers continues to find its way to the New World.

Kinderhook

Heading north on Route 9H, you will arrive at Kinderhook, which was first called *Kinderhoeck* (Children's corner) on a ca. 1616 map. Although it is likely that fur traders from Albany (*Beverwijck*) knew the isolated region well, settlement did not begin there until the late 1660s, after the first English victory in 1664. At the inland location where the King's Highway (linking Albany with Manhattan) met the "Great New England Path" (linking Albany with the Connecticut River Valley and Boston), the settlement became what is today the village of Kinderhook.

In this area the Dutch language was spoken into the 1840s, and the Dutch Reformed Church remained the only church in the community until almost 1830. At the time of the American Revolution, many Dutch families remained loyal to the English because the Dutch community had actually flourished under their rule. But some Dutch at Kinderhook supported the patriots.

Many travelers brought news of wartime developments to a tavern owned by Abraham and Maria Van Buren. Their oldest son, Martin Van Buren (1783–1863), the first president born in the new nation, grew up in an atmosphere of lively political discussion as the new government emerged. He was attracted to law, studied under local lawyers, and began his career in government in Kinderhook. (Van Buren is credited with popularizing the notion of "OK," meaning Old Kinderhook, which

Martin Van Buren, eighth President of the United States of America

he usually wrote after his name when signing his letters.) One of his mentors, Peter Van Ness, a Dutchman who had prospered during the war, had built a great mansion south of Kinderhook village in 1797. Forty or so years later, after Van Buren's term as the eighth president of the United States had ended, he returned to his native village and bought Van Ness's mansion and surrounding farmland to live on for the rest of his life.

Lindenwald

The house and grounds of **Lindenwald** are now a National Historic Site. Martin Van Buren's grave is in the village cemetery. The house in which Van Buren was born is no longer extant; its site is marked at the intersection of Broad Street (U.S. 9) and Hudson Street (County Route 21).

Route 9H/Old Post Road, near Albany Avenue about two miles south of Kinderhook
MAP 8 › E6

OPPOSITE AND ABOVE: Contemporary and historical images of Lindenwald, in Kinderhook, home of President Martin Van Buren

Luykas Van Alen House

Off Route 9H, about one mile south of Kinderhook Center
MAP 8 › E5

A well-restored structure still standing today south of Kinderhook village is the 18th-century **Luykas Van Alen House,** which represents traditional Dutch architecture with Dutch split doors and entrance stoops. There you can see how prosperous farm families of the second generation lived in the rural countryside. It is owned by the Columbia County Historical Society and is open to the public.

Turning south again from Kinderhook village and onto Route 26A, you will see views of an agricultural landscape with mountains in the background. This route leads to Stuyvesant Landing (the original Kinderhook Landing), about five miles to the west, where, despite its name, there is little left of the original Dutch settlement.

Crailo State Historic Site

9 1/2 Riverside Avenue, between Aiken Avenue and Belmore Place, now on the outskirts of Albany in Rensselaer
MAP 8 › E3

Heading towards Albany, you will find **Crailo State Historic Site,** an important museum that has been dedicated to the New Netherland history of the upper Hudson Valley. It includes a permanent exhibition called *A Sweet and Alien Land.* Originally part of the vast patroonship of Rensselaerswijck, Crailo was built in the early 18th century and remodeled in the Federal style

after the American Revolution. It houses furniture, glassware, pottery, and costumes from the Dutch period and is the only museum in North America devoted exclusively to 17th-century Dutch settlers.

Rensselaerswijck was the patroonship of the van Rensselaer family from Nijkerk and Amsterdam in the Dutch Republic. The original patroon, Kiliaen van Rensselaer (1595–1644), never visited his lands in America, but his sons managed its farms, fur trade, and commerce with New Amsterdam and later New York City. At one point Rensselaerswijck consisted of one million acres on both sides of the Hudson River.

Knickerbocker Historical Society

North of Albany, you will approach a village with the tongue-twisting name of Schaghticoke. Here the **Knickerbocker Historical Society** has restored and maintains the ca. 1770 Knickerbocker Mansion, of the real Knickerbocker family (not to be confused with Washington Irving's fictional Diedrich Knickerbocker). The historical society provides tours of the mansion, living history programs, and presentations on colonial New York, and holds several annual public events to raise funds for educational programming and restoration of the house.

132 Knickerbocker Road in Schaghticoke
MAP 8 › F1

Albany

Albany, the capital of New York State and one of the first regions in the United States to be settled by Europeans, is located 150 miles north of New York City and rests on the flood plain of the Hudson River. Here the river is an estuary, still part of the Atlantic Ocean, until it reaches Troy, just a few miles north of Albany on the river's eastern shore. Albany rises above the flood plain and spreads west for several miles on land formerly occupied by rich pine barrens. To the west of the city, the Helderberg Escarpment rises 1600 feet above sea level. To the east you can see the Rensselaer Escarpment, and to the north lie the Adirondack Mountains. When Henry Hudson reached the area in 1609, he remarked on its beauty.

Fort Nassau

Broadway
SUNY Central
Administration building
MAP 8 › E3

The first small fur-trading post, **Fort Nassau** on the tip of Castle Island, was flooded by freshets each year, and in 1624 Fort Orange was built nearby on the west shore of the Hudson River. It became the leading fur-trade center of North America during the 17th and 18th centuries, competing with the French and English trade centers in Canada and the Great Lakes region. The Dutch relationship with the Mahicans and Mohawks allowed them to prosper as thousands of beaver and other animal furs were shipped back to the Dutch Republic. A **commemorative plaque** on Broadway (SUNY Central Administration building) is all that remains of the old fort.

When New Netherland was taken over by the English in 1664, the settlement of *Beverwijck* that had developed around the fort was renamed "Albany," after the second title of the Duke of York. (The Dutch briefly regained their North American colony from August 1673 until ovember 1674, during which time they renamed Albany "*Willemstadt.*") Albany was chartered as a city in 1686, with Pieter Schuyler (1657–1724) as its first mayor.

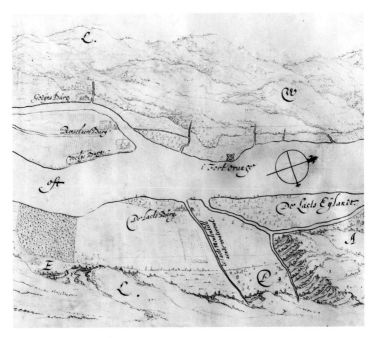

Map of the Rensselaerswijck
patroonship depicting Fort Orange,
1630 (detail) by Gillis van Scheyndel

It was in Albany that Benjamin Franklin delivered his Plan of Union in 1754 and the Continental Congress considered the first attempt to unite the colonies. The Act of Abjuration—the Dutch Republic's version of the Declaration of Independence—and the Dutch Union of Utrecht set general principles of provincial sovereignty that are similar to those found in the American Declaration of Independence and the Articles of Confederation. The great similarities prompted John Adams to write: "The origins of the two republics are so much alike that the history of one seems but a transcript from that of the other."

Today more than 25 percent of the population of Albany works in government-related jobs. It is a city filled with a diversity of architectural styles and unique streetscapes, but hardly any buildings of Dutch heritage remain, as the old city center was destroyed by modern urban renewal and neglect. During the late 19th and 20th centuries, entire blocks of homes and businesses were razed to build impressive government buildings like Albany's city hall, the state capitol building, and the Governor Nelson A. Rockefeller Empire State Plaza.

Tulip Festival

Washington Park between
Madison and Western
Avenues
MAP 8 › E3

Albany's "reinvented" Dutch cultural traditions
include the **Tulip Festival** each year in Washington
Park. This annual event marks the beginning of
spring as thousands of tulips bloom in the park
in early May. It includes musical performances,
vendors, and the coronation of the Tulip Queen.
Tulip Fest is the main celebration of the city's
rich Dutch heritage, but only one of many. It is
no wonder that one of Albany's baseball teams is
called the Dutchmen!

First Church of Albany

110 North Pearl Street
MAP 8 › E3

Founded in 1642, the **First Church of Albany,** a
descendant of the Reformed Protestant Dutch
Church, houses America's oldest existing pulpit,
hand-carved with its own hourglass, which was
imported from Holland in 1656 along with a
weathercock. The church is also the proud owner
of silver beakers from the Dutch period. The
current building was designed in 1798 by famed
architect Philip Hooker (1766–1836) and boasts
Tiffany-glass windows.

Quackenbush House

25 Quackenbush Square
MAP 8 › E3

The **Quackenbush House** was erected in the early
1700s in the Dutch vernacular style and has long
housed a restaurant. It is one of the oldest extant
buildings in the city of Albany. Originally the
house had a stepped front gable; it was modified
to its present Federal style sometime in the late
18th century by Colonel Hendrick Quackenbush
(1737–1813) when it was expanded as part of the
Quackenbush brick works located on the banks of
the Hudson River.

Dutch Art Collections

The **Albany Institute of History and Art,** founded in 1791, is dedicated to the history of the upper Hudson Valley. The museum is home to Dutch-related art and artifacts and hosts a replica of an early Dutch-style interior. The **New York State Museum,** housed in the Cultural Education Center, also has a small section (mainly archaeological) devoted to the Dutch heritage in Albany. Past archaeological excavations throughout the city have turned up various remains of the Native-American and Dutch colonial periods.

Albany Institute of
History and Art
125 Washington Avenue
MAP 8 › E3

New York State Museum
and Library
222 Madison Avenue
(housed in the Cultural
Education Center)
MAP 8 › E3

The Cultural Education Center also houses the **New York State Library,** where the New Netherland Institute, formerly called the New Netherland Project, has been diligently transcribing and translating the archives from the New Netherland period, a primary and major source of knowledge on the subject. Under the auspices of Dr. Charles Gehring, the early social, political, and economic life of the settler communities is being exhumed. These translations have been published in several volumes. In 2004 writer Russell Shorto brought this story to the broader public through his groundbreaking book on the founding of Dutch Manhattan, *The Island at the Center of the World*: *The Epic Story of Dutch Manhattan and the Forgotten Colony that Shaped America.*

Ten Broeck Mansion

The **Ten Broeck Mansion** was built in 1797–98 for General Abraham Ten Broeck (1734–1810) and his wife, Elizabeth Van Rensselaer (1734–1813), who named the Federal-style mansion "Prospect" because of its vantage point overlooking the Hudson Valley. The Ten Broeck family had already been in the New World for five generations when Abraham became a prosperous businessman and politician. In 1775 he was elected a delegate to the Second Continental Congress and two years later commanded the New York militia at the Battle of Saratoga as a brigadier general. From 1779 to 1783 he served both as mayor of

9 Ten Broeck Place
MAP 8 › E3

Albany and state senator. He was appointed the first judge of the Court of Common Pleas in 1781 by Governor George Clinton and served as the first president of the Bank of Albany. Ten Broeck only lived at Prospect for 12 years. The mansion, which has attractive period rooms and a recently rediscovered wine cellar, was given to the Albany Historical Association in 1942.

Schuyler Mansion

32 Catherine Street
MAP 8 › E3

The well-restored **Schuyler Mansion,** another historic site, was built in 1761 on 80 acres in the southern part of Albany known as the "Pastures" by General Philip Schuyler (1733–1804) when he married Catherine Van Rensselaer (1734–1803). Philip Schuyler was a soldier in the campaign against the French at Crown Point in 1755–56 and continued his military service for more than 20 years, eventually attaining the rank of major-general. He was also one of the first United States senators. On August 7, 1781, Native Americans and Loyalists raided his mansion in an unsuccessful attempt to kidnap Schuyler. A hatchet thrown by an Indian narrowly missed one of the Schuylers and lodged in a door frame, leaving a mark in the wood that can still be seen today. The Schuyler Mansion hosted many of the people who helped guide the young republic, including Benjamin Franklin, the Marquis de Lafayette, Count de Rochambeau, Baron Von Steuben, John Jay, Aaron Burr, George Washington, and Alexander Hamilton, who married Schuyler's daughter Elizabeth (Betsey) in 1780. After Philip Schuyler's death in 1804, the Schuyler estate was subdivided and sold off. The house remained a private residence for nearly 90 years; it then served as an orphanage until 1913 when it was purchased by the state of New York.

Historic Cherry Hill

Historic Cherry Hill was built in 1787 for Philip (1747–1798) and Maria Van Rensselaer (1749–1830). Comprising 900 acres, the site included a tannery and a brewery as well as a farm and was originally part of the Manor of Rensselaerwyck (now Rensselaer County), the vast tract of land owned by Kiliaen van Rensselaer. Philip Van Rensselaer, great-great grandson of the original patroon and a tenant on the farm, was elected the first supervisor of the new town of Bethlehem in 1794. Five generations of the Van Rensselaer family lived at Cherry Hill from 1787 until the death of the last descendant, Emily Rankin, in 1963. The house was opened as a museum in 1964 and is currently undergoing a long-term restoration project. Cherry Hill is also known for a murder: John Whipple was shot and killed there in 1827. John's wife, Elsie Lansing Whipple, and her lover, Jesse Strang, were tried for the murder. Elsie was acquitted, but Strang was sentenced to death and went down in history as the last man to be publicly hanged in Albany.

523 1/2 South Pearl Street
MAP 8 › E3

A replica of Henry Hudson's ship, **Halve Maen** (*Half Moon*), was built in Albany in 1989 on the initiative of Dr. Andy Hendricks to commemorate the Dutch role in exploring and colonizing America. Since then, the volunteer-based New Netherland Museum and skipper "Chip" Reynolds, who runs the ship, have been teaching all generations about the period of Dutch colonization and early sailing practices. Each year the ship traces part of Hudson's original route from New York City to Albany through a "voyage of discovery" with students from The Netherlands and the United States.

The First Jews in New Amsterdam

Paul Finkelman

When the Dutch West India Company (WIC) lost its toehold
in Brazil, many of the Dutch Jews who were living there fled.
Most went to the Dutch Republic, but in early September 1654,
23 Portuguese Jews from Recife arrived in New Amsterdam.
These refugees were not the first Jews to come to North America.
At least three—Jacob Barsimson, Solomon Pietersen, and Asser
Levy—had arrived earlier that summer directly from Amsterdam.
Ashkenazy Asser Levy would eventually become the leader of
the New Amsterdam and early New York Jewish community.
These first three Jews attracted little attention. The authorities
in New Netherland noted their arrival but did not seem disturbed
by their presence, perhaps because they arrived from the Dutch
Republic and had some assets. Furthermore, Barsimson was
apparently sent by the WIC itself. The 23 refugees from Recife,
however, received a different welcome. Petrus Stuyvesant
complained that the Jewish refugees would practice their
"customary usury and deceitful trading with the Christians." He
asked his superiors for permission to expel them. The directors
of the WIC shared some of Stuyvesant's concerns but refused
his request, pointing out that in Brazil Jews had suffered great
losses in the struggle against the Portuguese. A year later the
same directors reaffirmed that the Jews had "permission ... to
go to New Netherland and enjoy there the same privileges ... as
far as civil and political rights are concerned" that they had in
Amsterdam. They were barred from constructing a synagogue or
other place of public worship—something they lacked the funds to
do in any event—but they were allowed to build a cemetery and to
live peaceably in the community.

   Although the first Jewish congregation of New York, called
Shearith Israel, is thought to have been founded in 1654, the
earliest mention of Jewish worship dates to 1682. On a map from
1695 a rented synagogue is located on Beaver Street; five years
later the synagogue had moved to a house on Mill Street. Several
millstones from the old mill on that street have been found during
later excavations; two may be seen in the actual Shearith Israel

Beth Haim Cemetery, with the oldest
Jewish grave in New York, that of Benjamin
Bueno de Mesquita

synagogue at 8 West 77th Street, and another one was donated by
the synagogue to the West End Collegiate Church at 368 West End
Avenue at West 77th Street.

 The first "little hook of land" beyond the town wall that
Stuyvesant had designated as a Jewish cemetery disappeared
long ago. The oldest known Jewish grave in New York dates
from 1683 and belongs to Benjamin Bueno de Mesquita. It is in
a tiny cemetery, the Beth Haim cemetery of the Shearith Israel
congregation located on St. James Place, east of the Bowery in
Chinatown. The land had been purchased a year earlier by Iberian
Sephardic Jews who had emigrated to Amsterdam and then moved
to New York.

Schenectady

Located on the banks of the Mohawk River, 16 miles west of Albany, Schenectady (a Mohawk Indian word that means "beyond the pine plains") has played a significant role in American history—first as the westernmost and strategically and economically important Dutch settlement during the 17th and 18th centuries, and later as one of the wealthiest industrial cities in the United States.

Schenectady was founded in 1661 by 15 families from nearby Albany (*Beverwijck*), who subsequently built homes, barns, hay barracks, a Dutch Reformed church, a mill, and a brewery. Founder Arent Van Curler (1620–1667), from Nijkerk in the Dutch Republic, lived in the center of the new fortified village, while the other founding families settled on the remaining acres. Remarkably, many of the descendants of these families still live in the city where streets, schools, and other structures are named in their ancestors' honor.

The original village was laid out in a four-block area of about 20 acres surrounded in 1661 by a protective wooden palisade (the "stockade"), including a fortified blockhouse for soldiers. The streets were broad and perpendicular to each other, with 400 feet between the parallel streets. The blocks were divided into four lots of 200 feet, each having frontage on two streets. In addition to the village lots, every settling family was given a farm on the flats—or islands—along the Mohawk River, a piece of pasture land to the east of the village, and a garden to the south of the village.

During the Indian wars the Dutch were caught between English, French, and Indian interests. In the early morning hours of February 9, 1690, a band of French soldiers and their Indian allies from Canada attacked the sleeping village of Schenectady after frigid cold and deep snow forced them to abandon the idea of attacking Albany further to the east. In the fight Symon Schermerhorn watched as his son and three slaves were killed while he tried to defend his family. Wounded, he jumped on his horse and rode 16 miles through the cold winter night, alerting inhabitants as he passed through the outlying settlements. He reached Albany at 5 a.m., more dead than alive, warning of the impending invasion. When the two-hour massacre in Schenectady was over, 38 men, 10 women, and 12 children were dead. Twenty-seven others were taken prisoner and marched to Montreal, hundreds of miles to the north in Canada. Several of the prisoners were rescued,

The statue of Lawrence in the
Schenectady Stockade area (detail)

however, by Lawrence, a brave and noted Mohawk Indian, as his
warriors later pursued and caught up with the fleeing French. A statue
in Lawrence's honor was erected in the late 19th century and now
serves as the centerpiece of the Stockade area. The survivors of the
Schenectady Massacre built a new stockade, and within eight years
more than 130 homes and businesses had replaced the fallen village.
While hostilities continued in the surrounding countryside for years,
Schenectady was never attacked again.

Schenectady entered the 18th century as a mercantile and
shipbuilding community. After the 1825 opening of the Erie Canal,
which stretched from Albany to Buffalo, Schenectady became a center
of industrial innovation as Thomas Edison, George Westinghouse, and
the Schenectady Locomotive Company made Schenectady the city
that "Lights and Hauls the World."

Schenectady County Historical Society

32 Washington Avenue
MAP 8 › D2

The original dimensions of Schenectady's Stockade area are still more or less intact. You can get some sense of what it was like during the 17th century by walking the city's stockade streets and admiring its architecture, some of which dates back to the early days of Dutch settlement. The local Dutch Reformed Church played a major role in providing for the religious and social needs of the inhabitants. The **Schenectady County Historical Society** owns an 1843 painting of the Dutch Reformed church at the intersection of South Church Street with Union Street. After the burning of the first church during the massacre of 1690, a new one was built in 1703 on the site of the first structure. It was abandoned in 1734 and used as a fort until a new church was built. In front of the church, several Schenectady residents erected a Liberty Pole and flag in 1774 to protest English rule and to support independence. After 1814 the church was rebuilt at its present location slightly northeast of the earlier site. That church burned in 1948 but was restored as the present structure, including a stained-glass window with the Dutch motto of the Reformed Church in America: "*eendracht maakt macht*" ("in unity there is strength"). The door on its east side faces Holland and is still called "forefathers entrance."

Across from the church, attached to the Stockade Inn (1 North Church Street), is a **plaque** commemorating Schenectady's founder, Arent van Curler. A corresponding plaque was erected in his native town, Nijkerk, in The Netherlands, which still has a regular exchange with Schenectady.

Dutch Stockade Houses

Isaac Vrooman House
31 Front Street
MAP 8 › D2

Built in 1754, the privately owned **Isaac Vrooman House** is a rare example of a Dutch townhouse. Isaac Vrooman (1721–1807) lived here until 1759. He was a large landowner and prominent citizen of Schenectady who made several maps of the Schenectady area, including one for George

Washington. He was a member of the General Assembly in 1759–1761, later a member of the New York State Assembly, and was appointed mayor of Schenectady in 1765. This house is almost identical to another privately owned house nearby at **29 Front Street,** a Dutch-style house that still had its original iron lintels in the 1930s. The gable trim remains intact, but the construction date, "AD 1754," located below the attic window, has been removed. The **Johannes Teller House,** built in 1740, is another early example of a Dutch house in Schenectady. Johannes Teller (1659–1725) was the son of Willem Teller (ca. 1620–ca. 1701), one of the city's founders.

Abraham Yates lived at **109 Union Street** in a classic Dutch-American gable-end house, built in 1730. It has characteristic fleur-de-lis wall tiles, as well as Dutch brick bond; it was also originally furnished with a jambless fireplace.

The **Hendrick Brouwer House** was built prior to 1700 and is said to include a secret underground passage to the river. The house is privately owned.

29 Front Street
MAP 8 › D2

Johannes Teller House
(below)
121 Front Street
MAP 8 › D2

Dutch-American gable-end house
109 Union Street
MAP 8 › D2

Hendrick Brouwer House
14 North Church Street
MAP 8 › D2

The Abraham Yates House on Union Street

Mabee Farm

1080 Main Street in
Rotterdam Junction
MAP 8 › C1

Early Dutch history survives outside the city as well. The **Mabee Farm** is the oldest extant structure in the entire Mohawk Valley in New York State. It contains many interesting original furnishings, tools, and family papers. Originally settled through a deed from English Governor Francis Lovelace (1621–1675) to Daniel Janse van Antwerpen (1635–1715) in 1671, it was the site of a fur-trading post where Native-American traders could be intercepted before they arrived at the village of Schenectady. In 1706 van Antwerpen sold the western portion of his land to Jan Pieterse Mabee, and it remained in the Mabee family for 287 years. The farm includes a stone gable-end farmhouse with a jambless fireplace, brick slave quarters, and a wood-framed inn that served early travelers in the Mohawk Valley before the advent of the Erie Canal in 1825. The Mabee family cemetery lies just a few feet from the farmhouse and contains graves that date back to the early 1700s. The farm originally included Dutch barns, but they were destroyed by fire in the 20th century. They were replaced by the ca. 1760 Dutch barn that was moved here from its original Johnstown, New York, site in 1999. At 54 feet by 52 feet, the barn is exceptionally large and

is used for workshops, historical reenactments, educational programs, and displays.

The farm was also recently the site of construction of a **replica of the *Onrust***, the ship built in 1614 by Dutch captain Adriaen Block and his crew after his own ship, the *Tijger*, had burned. The *Onrust* made exploratory voyages up and down the Atlantic seaboard and allowed Block to draw a reliable map of part of the east coast, subsequently claiming it for the Dutch Republic. From 2006 to 2009 more than 250 volunteers built the 52-foot-long *Onrust* replica using 17th-century Dutch shipbuilding techniques. The *Onrust* replica is being used to teach early Dutch and maritime history throughout the Northeast.

Homes with Dutch Ancestry

The privately owned **Arent Bradt Residence,** just outside the small town of Rotterdam, was built in 1736 and is a very good example of a Dutch farmhouse of the period. Arent Bradt, the builder of the house, was related to a Norwegian brewmaster of the same name who was the first settler in the region in 1662 and was killed in the 1690 massacre. Other examples of farmhouses in the area with Dutch-period ancestry are the **Schermerhorn Homestead** and the **Dellemont-Wemple Farm,** both also privately owned.

Arent Bradt Residence
22 Schermerhorn Road
near Rotterdam
MAP 8 › D2

Schermerhorn Homestead
47 Schermerhorn Road
near Rotterdam
MAP 8 › D2

Dellemont-Wemple Farm
268 Wemple Road
near Rotterdam
MAP 8 › D2

West of the Hudson River

TRAVELING SOUTH

As you drive south from Albany along Route 87 (New York State Thruway), you should try to take small detours to the former Dutch settlements. Even though the remnants are scattered and few, they provide charming encounters with the past. Route 9W, which is closer to the river, is an even better choice for a drive, as it essentially follows the old road south.

Dutch Houses in Coeymans

Ariaantje Coeymans Stone House
28 Stonehouse Hill Road
MAP 8 › E5

Tobias Ten Eyk House and Cemeteries
On the Old Ravena Road, north of the Route 9W junction
MAP 8 › E5

The first village on your way south, off Route 87 towards the Hudson River, is Coeymans, named after early settler Barent Pietersz Coeymans who arrived as an apprentice at the local grist mill of the Van Rensselaers. In the early 1670s he purchased land from the Indians, known later as the Coeymans Patent. The oldest remaining houses are the **Ariaantje Coeymans Stone House,** built ca. 1716 at the north end of the village, and the **Tobias Ten Eyk House and cemeteries.** Both houses are privately owned.

Bronck Museum

Route 9W on Pieter Bronck Road in Coxsackie
MAP 8 › E6

Just south of the center of Coxsackie at Plank Road, along Route 9W you will find the **Bronck Museum,** operated by the Green House Historical Society since 1939 and occupying a farm that was in the Bronck family for eight generations. The oldest structure on the farm, a one-room stone dwelling, was built by Pieter Bronck in 1663 and is the oldest surviving house in the upper Hudson area. Other structures include a larger house built by Pieter's grandson in 1738 and a "New World" Dutch barn. All structures house collections of 18th- and 19th-century family furniture, regional art, textiles, and household furnishings.

Catskill

Catskill, a creek and village better known for the mountain range of the same name to the west, is complemented by another nearby creek, appropriately called Katerskill (a *kater* is a tomcat in Dutch). Names can be deceptive, as Catskill is most likely named for an Indian sachem. The popular mountain range was immortalized in Washington Irving's story of Rip Van Winkle, who overslept his time somewhere in those mountains.

Kiersted House Museum

Further south you will arrive at Saugerties. The origin of this charming town's name has sometimes been attributed to *zagertje* (the little sawyer), a reference to one of its first inhabitants, Arent Cornelissen Vogel, who apparently operated a small mill in the area. Another suggested origin, *zagerskilletje,* refers not only to the sawyer, but also to his location at a *kill* (body of water).

119 Main Street
in Saugerties
MAP 7 › E2

The **Kiersted House Museum,** built in the early 18th century and once the home of John Kiersted (1786–1862), a member of a prominent family in Ulster County, dates back to the colonial period. It is now home to the Saugerties Historical Society.

Kingston

Wiltwijck, New Netherland's third major settlement after New Amsterdam and present-day Albany, is known today as Kingston. Unlike New York City and Albany, where traces from colonial times may be difficult to find, in Kingston there is more evidence of the history of Dutch colonization. Although the Stockade area, which protected Dutch settlers against Indian attacks like the one in Schenectady, has disappeared, its ground plan is still traceable in the layout of the streets. In 1652 approximately 60–70 settlers moved south from Fort Orange to the fertile flood plains of the Esopus Creek, north of the location where the Rondout Creek meets the Hudson River. This brought them close to the Esopus Indians, the original inhabitants of the area. Land disputes led the two sides to the brink of war, with both the Europeans and the Indians engaging in petty vandalism and kidnapping. In 1657 Director General Stuyvesant sent soldiers north from New Amsterdam to defend the colonists and help build a stockade around 40 houses. The settlers took down their barns and houses board by board and carted them uphill to a bluff overlooking the Esopus Creek. They reconstructed their homes behind a 14-foot-high wall made of tree trunks pounded into the ground that created a perimeter approximately 1200 feet by 1300 feet. By day the men left their walled village to go out and farm their fields, while women and children remained largely confined within the stockade. The villagers lived this way until 1664, when a peace treaty ended the conflict with the Esopus Indians.

Old Dutch Church Heritage Museum

272 Wall Street
in Kingston
MAP 7 › D3

Organized as a congregation in 1659, the **Old Dutch Church Heritage Museum** is Kingston's oldest institution. The churchyard contains numerous beautifully carved early Dutch gravestones, as well as the grave of George Clinton, New York's first governor.

Hoffman House Restaurant

The **Hoffman House Restaurant** is located in the Stockade area. Musket holes found in the upper floor and attic steps leading to the roof suggest its possible early use as a fort or lookout. Today this building, which is listed on the National Register of Historic Places, is a restaurant with cozy fireside seating in the winter months and a lovely open-air patio for visitors to enjoy in the warmer months.

94 North Front Street in Kingston
MAP 7 › D3

Senate House

The New York State Senate convened its first meeting in the **Senate House** while it was the home of Abraham Van Gaasbeek (1718–1797). Built in 1676, the stone house reflects the building traditions of the original Dutch colonists as well as the gradual adoption of English construction techniques. The adjacent museum contains the largest American collection of paintings, drawings, and papers of John Vanderlyn (1775–1852), a well-known painter of Dutch descent who worked in the early 19th century. Concerts, lectures, and major events are offered by the museum throughout the year.

296 Fair Street at North Front Street and Clinton Avenue in Kingston
MAP 7 › D3

Hurley Heritage Society Museum

52 Main Street in Hurley
MAP 7 › D3

Hurley, a pretty village west of Kingston and Route 87, has several old stone houses, many with a Dutch architectural or historic legacy. It was first settled in 1662 by five men from Albany, who named it New Village *(Nieuw Dorp)*. Hurley's Main Street is a National Historic Landmark District. The **Hurley Heritage Society Museum** holds various displays about the town, changing exhibits of historical interest, and a gift shop which includes Delft ceramics.

Bevier House Museum

2682 Route 209
in Marbletown
MAP 7 › D4

Southwest of Hurley is Marbletown, which hosts the **Bevier House Museum/Ulster County Historical Society.** Built in the 1680s as a one-room Dutch dwelling, the building now displays the history of the Hudson Valley and its inhabitants, housing collections of 18th- and 19th-century furniture, decorative arts, and tools.

Klyne Esopus Historical Society Museum

Back on Route 9W, south of Kingston is Esopus, named after the local Indian tribe, possibly by the Dutch. The town boasts the **Klyne Esopus Historical Society Museum,** housed in a former Dutch Reformed church that was established in 1791 and built in its present form in 1827.

764 Broadway/Route 9W in Esopus
MAP 7 › E4

New Paltz

The story of New Paltz began more than four centuries ago along today's borders of France and Belgium. At that time the Wars of Religion were raging throughout northern Europe, and the region's French-speaking Protestants, known as Walloons, and other future New Paltz families found temporary refuge in the Palatine-Rhine region in southwestern Germany. This area, as well as the Dutch Republic, had long served as a sanctuary for foreign Protestants. However, fear of the plague and of French invasion caused some religious refugees to cross the Atlantic with other Dutch and French-speaking settlers.

More Huguenots and Walloons arrived during the 1660s and 1670s. In 1677, twelve men from this group met with five Esopus leaders to negotiate the purchase of 40,000 acres of land on the west bank of the

Wallkill River that was to become the New Paltz Patent. In exchange, the Huguenots paid the Esopus with a collection of goods that included, as was usual at the time, farming tools, clothing, blankets, wine, horses, tobacco, gunpowder, and lead. The location of the village, which had been a Native-American campsite for centuries, was situated above the flood level, near rich farmlands and woodlots. The settlers soon cleared the land for farming and constructed temporary dwellings. Thus New Paltz came into being. Through intermarriage New Paltz's population rapidly became an ethnic mix of French and Dutch. Before long the two groups would become so intertwined they were almost indistinguishable. By 1790 the population had grown to over 2,000 inhabitants, including English, Scottish, and Irish immigrants, and enslaved Africans.

Historic Huguenot Street

Huguenot Street
in New Paltz
MAP 7 › D5

Historic Huguenot Street, with seven original stone houses dating to the early 1700s, a cemetery, and a reconstructed stone church built in 1717, survives today as one of the most significant and comprehensive collections of early colonial architecture in the United States. Visitors to New Paltz can tour houses whose interiors represent different time periods—a unique opportunity to trace the community as it developed over 300 years.

DuBois Fort

Huguenot Street
in New Paltz
MAP 7 › D5

The first building, **DuBois Fort**, built in 1705, protected citizens from possible invasion. Two portholes may still be seen on the east side of the house. Today the house serves as the **Historic Huguenot Street Visitor Center** with a museum shop, rotating exhibits, and a tour office.

Dutch Reformed Church in New Netherland and in British Colonial America

Francis J. Sypher

In 1628 Jonas Michaëlius, the first Dutch Protestant minister in New Netherland, arrived in New Amsterdam and assumed leadership of the Dutch Reformed Church congregation that eventually became the Collegiate Churches of New York. Other congregations of the Reformed Church were subsequently organized in Albany (*Beverwijck*), on Long Island, along the Hudson River, and in New Jersey south to the Delaware River.

Religion was vitally important to the early Dutch settlers, as well as to Huguenots and others. Many early settlers were devout believers in the Bible and in sin and salvation. It was thought that religion could help structure the young and diverse settler society. Thus, the *domines* (sometimes spelled *dominies*), or Protestant ministers, quickly became pivotal, sometimes controversial, figures in the new colony's society.

The Dutch Reformed Church was established as the public church in New Netherland (as it was in the Dutch Republic), and it grew rapidly. In keeping with the Dutch policy of freedom of conscience, people of other beliefs were, on the whole, allowed to practice their religion in private, although not in public religious gatherings. By the mid-1650s New Netherland had become a religiously diverse community, including English Puritans, Jews, Lutherans, Mennonites, Quakers, Roman Catholics, and others.

After 1664 when the English took control of the colony, the Church of England was established in New York, but the Dutch were allowed to continue public practice of their own religion. The Dutch Reformed Church flourished until the early 1700s, mainly through natural growth—colonial families often included 10 or more children. But immigration from New England and from England, Germany, and other parts of Europe brought newcomers with other religious views. As the Dutch language declined in use, the Reformed Church gradually began to hold services in English; by the early 19th century, all services were in English. At the same time, the Dutch Reformed Church underwent movements

to establish independent church government, separating it from the Amsterdam classis, and to develop schools that could train ministers in America. After the American Revolution, the Dutch Reformed Church, later named the Reformed Church in America, became truly independent.

The first Dutch church building in New Amsterdam was built in 1633 on Pearl Street. In 1642 a new church was erected inside the fort at the tip of Manhattan. Under the English this church was also used for Anglican worship. The Dutch congregation eventually built their own church on Garden Street (later renamed Exchange Place). It was built of stone and wood and completed by 1695, rebuilt in 1807, and destroyed by fire in 1835. There were also Dutch Reformed churches in Harlem, Brooklyn, Albany, Kingston, Hackensack (New Jersey), and elsewhere, often built on octagonal plans following Dutch tradition.

Still standing today is the historic Dutch church at Sleepy Hollow, dating from 1685, and made famous by Washington Irving in "The Legend of Sleepy Hollow." Most of the original Dutch churches in Brooklyn, the Hudson Valley, and New Jersey have been replaced by later buildings, but their cemeteries often still include typical red sandstone gravestones marked with family names and commemorative texts in Dutch—silent witnesses of the past.

OPPOSITE: Saddle River Reformed Church, Upper Saddle River
ABOVE: Interior of the Old Dutch Church, Sleepy Hollow

Jean Hasbrouck House

Huguenot Street
in New Paltz
MAP 7 › D5

To the north you will find the **Jean Hasbrouck House,** which was built in 1712. Its current appearance, with its four-room plan and central hallway, was completed by Jean Hasbrouck's son Jacob in 1721. Only the original chimney on the west side of the house represents clear evidence of the earlier structure. The jambless fireplace added in 1721 remains in the kitchen and is one of the few surviving fireplaces of its type in the United States.

Bevier-Elting House

Huguenot Street
in New Paltz
MAP 7 › D5

Three hundred feet farther north, close to the Historic Huguenot Street Library and Archives, is the **Bevier-Elting House**. Its three-room plan was completed in 1735, although it is likely that the house was built earlier as a simpler structure. The house also includes an external shed-roof passageway (*uitlaet*) and an unusual sub-cellar used for storage.

Ezekiel Elting House

The **Ezekiel Elting House**, built in 1799, is of a Federal design that contrasts with the earlier stone houses. Ezekiel, a prosperous area merchant, took advantage of the clear view from the Wallkill River to show off his attractive new house with its symmetrical design, brick facade, and front-room store.

Huguenot Street
in New Paltz
MAP 7 › D5

Deyo House

The **Deyo House** was probably built by Pierre Deyo as a simple stone structure similar to the other homes on Huguenot Street. In 1894 Abraham Deyo Brodhead (1862–1926) and his wife, Gertrude Deyo, commissioned architect Whether Beardsley to expand the Deyos' stone house into a large Queen Anne-style home with a portico, a whitewashed faux-fireplace, and forced-hot-air radiators with copper piping.

Huguenot Street
in New Paltz
MAP 7 › D5

Abraham Hasbrouck House

The **Abraham Hasbrouck House** was constructed by Abraham's son, Daniel Hasbrouck (d. 1759), building on the pre-existing basement left by his father. The house was unusual for Dutch colonial construction: typically, the gable side of the house faced the road, but here Daniel ran the roof line parallel to the road. The house remained in the family through the 19th century. It has been restored to the building's 18th-century appearance.

Huguenot Street
in New Paltz
MAP 7 › D5

Freer House

The **Freer House** was built in 1762–1763 by Johannes Low (b. 1715) and Rebecca Freer, who incorporated portions of an earlier wood-frame house that was probably built by Rebecca's father, Hugo Freer. Successive owners made numerous changes to the house.

Huguenot Street
in New Paltz
MAP 7 › D5

Old Huguenot Burial Ground

Huguenot Street
in New Paltz
MAP 7 › D5

The original stone church (the "French Church")
was erected in 1717, replacing an earlier wood
church. The community dismantled the structure
in 1772 when they built a larger church up the
street (the site of the current congregation). In
1972 the Crispell Family Association and Historic
Huguenot Street reconstructed the 1717 church,
which now serves as a public museum and
a venue for weddings, concerts, and special
events. The adjacent **Old Huguenot Burial
Ground** contains several classic examples of early
American gravestone art. The earliest surviving
gravestone dates from 1724, and the last stone is
dated 1861.

Hasbrouck House

84 Liberty Street
in Newburgh
MAP 7 › D1

Newburgh, further south on Route 87, was
settled in the 18th century by Germans from the
Palatine-Rhine region, although little is left of
their legacy. George Washington's longest stay
at a Revolutionary War headquarters occurred
here at the **Hasbrouck House,** the Hasbrouck
family's 1727 Dutch vernacular stone farmhouse
overlooking the Hudson River. It is a New York
State Historic Site and the first public historic
site in the United States.

Dutch Reformed Church

The city of Newburgh, together with the World Monuments Fund and other donors, is currently restoring the **Dutch Reformed Church,** an important Gothic Revival building designed by Alexander Jackson Davis (1803–1892) in 1835.

134 Grand Street near Montgomery Street in Newburgh
MAP 7 › D1

Jacob Blauvelt House

In New City, Rockland County, you will find the **Jacob Blauvelt House.** Home of the **Rockland County Historical Society**, this two-story, gambrel-roofed, brick farmhouse was built in 1832 by one of the county's founding families and is a good local example of Dutch-Flemish architecture. The house includes six period rooms with Hudson Valley furnishings and has an adjacent historic barn and carriage house.

20 Zukor Road in New City
MAP 7 › E4

DeWint House

The town of Tappan is the site of another outstanding example of Dutch colonial architecture in the Hudson Valley: the **DeWint House,** the oldest surviving structure in Rockland County, which was built in 1700 and named after the family that owned it during George Washington's visits. The town served as Washington's temporary headquarters on four separate occasions during the Revolutionary War and hosted the famous treason trial of the British spy, Major John André. Tappan has a number of historic houses, including the **Manse** and the **Mabie Houses**, and hosts occasional commemorative events.

110 Main Street in Tappan
MAP 7 › E5

New Jersey
and Delaware

The land claimed by the Dutch, based on Henry Hudson's 1609 voyage and later called New Netherland, encompassed the eastern seaboard of the United States from the Connecticut River to the Delaware River. Dutch settlements in present-day New Jersey and Delaware were sparse in the New Netherland period, limited to a few small towns and scattered farmsteads. However, there is a wealth of post-New Netherland-period sites, especially in northern New Jersey, and thus we recommend a visit to historic sites in both New Jersey and Delaware for a true sense of the Dutch presence in this area. Both states boast Dutch-American farmhouses and farm buildings, open to the public and privately owned, as well as historical markers of significance to the Dutch history of the area.

This chapter will take you to several counties (in particular, Hudson, Monmouth, Bergen, Passaic, Middlesex, Somerset, Sussex, and Warren) and to the Delaware Water Gap in New Jersey. In Delaware the tour visits Lewes and other Delaware River towns. Sites are far flung, and traveling by car—ideally with a GPS device—is a must if you wish to see them. We have provided some general directions to guide you within counties, but you will need your own map or navigational guide to find individual sites. A less ambitious approach would be to focus your visit on Bergen or Middlesex and Somerset Counties in New Jersey or Lewes in Delaware, each of which holds a variety of significant sites related to the Dutch legacy.

OPPOSITE: Headstone at the Blauvelt
Cemetery, Harrington Park, NJ

New Jersey

The only Dutch settlements in New Jersey during the New Netherland period comprised the patroonship of Pavonia (in what is today Jersey City), a couple of agricultural towns (Bergen, Hoboken), and several dispersed farms. Most Dutch settlements in this area date from after the English conquest of New Netherland in 1664. Many were actually secondary settlements by Dutch families from Long Island and Manhattan, escaping the battlefields of the American Revolution. They settled along the Hackensack and Saddle River valleys in Bergen County, the Passaic River valley in Passaic County, the Raritan River valley in Middlesex and Somerset Counties, and in Monmouth County across the lower New York Harbor from Brooklyn. Many Jersey-Dutch families were farmers and became major slaveholders in 18th-century New Jersey. Remnants of the Jersey-Dutch dialect continued into the first decades of the 20th century.

The Jersey Dutch had a lasting impact on the regional architecture, fostering what has become known as the Dutch-American or Dutch colonial farmhouse, with its distinctive gambrel roofs. A surprising number of Dutch-American farmhouses, Dutch Reformed churches, and Dutch barns remain as visible reminders of the Dutch colonial culture in New Jersey.

OPPOSITE: Historical Marker, Jersey City, 2010

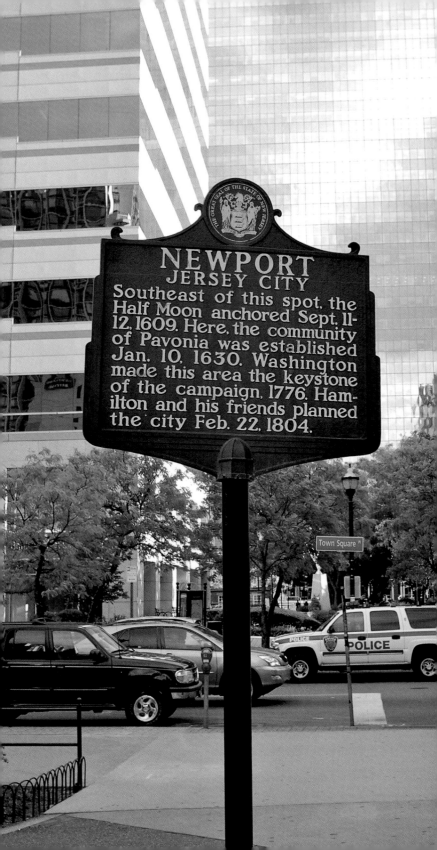

NEWPORT
JERSEY CITY
Southeast of this spot, the Half Moon anchored Sept. 11-12, 1609. Here, the community of Pavonia was established Jan. 10, 1630. Washington made this area the keystone of the campaign, 1776. Hamilton and his friends planned the city Feb. 22, 1804.

MAP 9
Northern New Jersey
Bergen and Passaic Counties

RAMAPO RIVER

ROUTE 202

I-287

• Laroe-Van Horn House

• Mahwah

Upper Saddle River •
Saddle River Reformed Church
Hopper-Goetschius House
Van Riper-Tice Barn

Hendrick Van Allen House
•

Saddle River •

•
Oakland
Jacobus S.
Demarest House

• Wyckoff
Van Voorhees-Quackenbush-Zabriskie House
Wyckoff Reformed Church

SADDLE RIVER R

ROUTE 17

• Wayne
Dey Mansion
Schuyler Colfax House
Van Riper-Hopper House
Mead-Van Duyne House

ROUTE 208

ROUTE 23

PASSAIC RIVER

Fairlawn •
Garretson Forge and Farm

Paterson ■

I-80

GARDEN STATE PKWY

Clifton
Hamilton-Van
Wagoner House

• Passaic

A   B   C

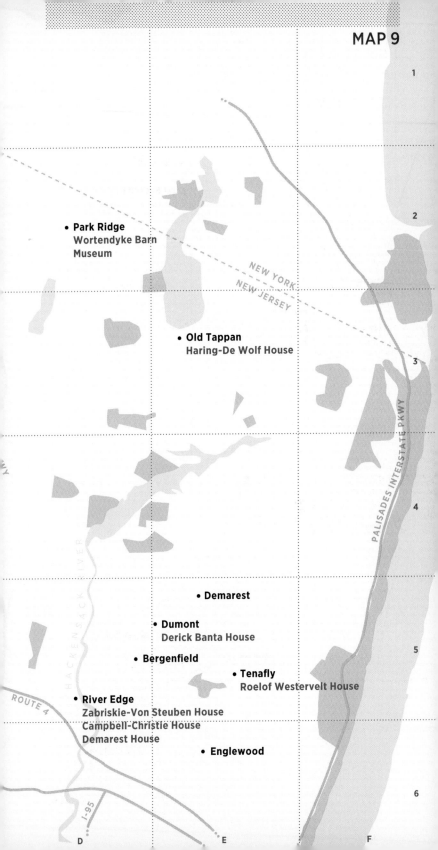

MAP 9

1

2

• **Park Ridge**
Wortendyke Barn
Museum

NEW YORK
NEW JERSEY

• **Old Tappan**
Haring-De Wolf House

3

PALISADES INTERSTATE PKWY

4

HACKENSACK RIVER

• **Demarest**

• **Dumont**
Derick Banta House

5

• **Bergenfield**

• **Tenafly**
Roelof Westervelt House

ROUTE 4

• **River Edge**
Zabriskie-Von Steuben House
Campbell-Christie House
Demarest House

• **Englewood**

6

I-95

D   E   F

Northern New Jersey

Bergen County

Bergen County has a strong Dutch legacy and an impressive number of Dutch colonial houses. Director General Petrus Stuyvesant and his council granted a charter to the village of Bergen in 1661, thereby establishing the oldest municipality in what is now New Jersey. Bergen County, however, is located to the north of that former village.

🚗 You can start this tour at River Edge and work your way through Bergen County, visiting sites that interest you. The houses are described in roughly counter-clockwise order, but it is probably not possible to visit them all in one day.

Zabriskie-Von Steuben House

1209 Main Street
in River Edge
MAP 9 › D5

In River Edge at Historic New Bridge Landing, once a prosperous mill site on the Hackensack River, three historic houses are located close together. The land on which the **Zabriskie-Von Steuben House** (also known as the **Von Steuben House**) is located was owned by David Ackerman, who came to New Amsterdam from Blaricum in the Dutch Republic in 1664. He resettled with his family in the village of Hackensack in 1686. His son, Johannes Ackerman (b. 1684), built a grist mill on the banks of the river. In the 1740s the county of Bergen built a wood drawbridge across the river, which provided the town with the name New Bridge. In 1745 the Ackermans sold the grist mill to Jan (or John) Zabriski(e) (1716–1774), whose grandfather Albrecht Zaborowski migrated to New Netherland from Prussia in 1662. Jan Zabriski(e) probably built the oldest section of the house in 1752 and then enlarged his dwelling around 1767 from five to twelve rooms, warmed by seven fireplaces and covered by a gambrel roof.

New Bridge was an important location where the Continental Army crossed the Hackensack River after the British conquest of Fort Lee in

November 1776. After Jan Zabriski(e) sided with the British, the house was confiscated by the state of New Jersey and awarded in 1783 to Baron Friedrich Von Steuben (1730–1794), a Prussian officer who had trained the Continental Army at Valley Forge during the winter of 1777–1778. However, Von Steuben only stayed occasionally in the house and sold it again in 1788. Today, it is the headquarters of the **Bergen County Historical Society,** a museum with Bergen-Dutch furnishings, run by the Historic New Bridge Landing Park Commission.

Campbell-Christie House

The **Campbell-Christie House** was built by Jacob Campbell, a mason, ca. 1774. Jacob was the son of Willem Campbell, an Ulster Scot, who married French Huguenot Elizabeth De Marest of Schraalenburgh (an area that now includes Dumont and Bergenfield) and owned 33 acres of improved land in the Old Bridge section of what was then Hackensack Township. The red sandstone house with a center hall and a gambrel roof was originally located in New Milford. In 1977 it was moved to its present location on land owned by the Bergen County Historical Society. Restored as a late-18th-century tavern, it is open for special events.

1201 Main Street
in River Edge
MAP 9 › D5

Demarest House

Main Street in River Edge
MAP 9 › D5

The nearby **Demarest House** (directly behind the Zabriskie-Von Steuben House) was probably built by Jacobus Paulison, who purchased 100 acres of land from Jacob Demarest in 1791, erected a gristmill on the Hackensack River, and built this two-room house for his son-in-law shortly after his marriage in 1794. It was originally located near the Old French Burying Ground and was moved to its present location in 1955–1956 and restored by the Blauvelt-Demarest Foundation. The site is open to the public for special events.

Dutch-American Style Houses

Derick Banta House
180 Washington Avenue
in Dumont, formerly
Schraalenburg
MAP 9 › D5

Roelof Westervelt House
(below)
256 Tenafly Road near
Westervelt Avenue in
Tenafly
MAP 9 › E5

Haring-De Wolf House
95 De Wolf Road in Old
Tappan
MAP 9 › E3

Farther east and northeast, somewhat closer to the New York State border and the Palisades Interstate Parkway, you will find other good examples of the Dutch-American style. The **Derick Banta House** today houses the Dixon Homestead Library, built in 1780–1790. (Dumont also has an Old North Reformed church and an old slave cemetery). The **Roelof Westervelt House,** built in 1798, and the **Haring-De Wolf House,** built ca. 1720, are private residences.

Although it has few sites dating back to the New Netherland period, the northern section of Bergen County boasts the largest and richest variety of historic buildings, houses, barns, and churches associated with the Dutch in New Jersey and possibly in the United States, belonging to families like the Bantas, Van Horns, Westervelts, Blauvelts, Harings, and Demarests. The sites are too numerous to be covered in this guide, but it is worthwhile to check them out on bergencountyhistory.org or other links cited in the Appendix.

Garretson Forge and Farm

4–02 River Road
in Fair Lawn
MAP 9 › C5

North of River Edge, on River Road in Fair Lawn, between the Passaic and Saddle Rivers, is the **Garretson Forge and Farm.** In 1719 Gerrit Gerritse purchased land between these rivers as part of the Saddle River Patent. His son Peter built the red sandstone farmhouse, which originally had a pitched roof, later modified into a gambrel roof. Today the house and several outbuildings are open as a small museum.

Wortendyke Barn Museum

In Park Ridge the exhibitions of the **Wortendyke Barn Museum** include handmade 18th- and 19th-century farm implements and tools and tell the history of the Wortendyke family farm and the agricultural development of Bergen County from the first settlement to the present.

13 Pascack Road in Park Ridge
MAP 9 › D2

Saddle River Reformed Church

Known as the "Old Stone Church," the **Saddle River Reformed Church** was organized in 1784. It was originally a "daughter church" of the Paramus Reformed Church. In 1811, however, the Saddle River Reformed Church split from the mother church because its congregation preferred to conduct services in English. Most Dutch Reformed

500 East Saddle River Road, at Old Stone Church Road in Upper Saddle River
MAP 9 › C2

churches in Bergen County continued to use Dutch for afternoon services through the 1870s. The present church was built in 1819 and was renovated in 1971–1972.

Hopper-Goetschius House and Van Riper-Tice Barn

245 Lake Street in
Upper Saddle River
MAP 9 › C2

The oldest section of the red sandstone, Dutch-American **Hopper-Goetschius House** was built by the Hopper family in 1739; the main section with a gambrel roof was completed prior to 1800. In 1814 the Reverend Stephen Goetschius (1752–1837), the pastor of the Old Stone Church, purchased the house. It remained in the Goetschius family until 1985, when it was donated to the borough of Upper Saddle River for use as a museum by the Upper Saddle River Historical Society. Many of its artifacts, including kitchen tools, furniture, quilts, china, and glass, were the property of the Goetschius family.

In 1989 the Upper Saddle River Historical Society also acquired the **Van Riper-Tice Barn**, a Dutch barn with an H-bent frame, and moved it from its original location on West Saddle River Road to this site. The barn contains a large collection of farm tools, wagons, and sleighs.

Ramapo Valley

In Mahwah, close to Ramapo College, stands the 1750 **Laroe-Van Horn House,** built on the estate of early industrialist Theodore Havemeyer.

In the Ramapo Valley in Oakland**,** you will encounter more Dutch colonial houses: the **Hendrick Van Allen House** was built before the American Revolution and served as a headquarters for George Washington in 1777.

Further along Ramapo Valley Road, another historic house, also privately owned, is the **Jacobus S. Demarest House** built around 1789.

In the Ramapo Mountains resides a group of descendants of a free Afro-Dutch population, who became some of the first black landowners in America in 1681 when they purchased shares in the Tappan Patent in the upper Hackensack Valley. Although many have Dutch-sounding surnames (De Groat, De Freese, Van Dunk), they incorporated themselves into a Native-American tribe in 1978.

Laroe-Van Horn House
398 Ramapo Valley Road
in Mahwah
MAP 9 › B1

Hendrick Van Allen House
3–15 Ramapo Valley Road
(U.S. 202) at Franklin
Avenue in Oakland
MAP 9 › A3

Jacobus S. Demarest House
3 Dogwood Drive
in Oakland
MAP 9 › A3

ABOVE: Laroe-Van Horn House
LEFT: Hendrick Van Allen House (detail)

Wyckoff

**Van Voorhees-
Quackenbush-
Zabriskie House**
421 Franklin Avenue
at Maple Avenue in Wyckoff
MAP 9 › A3

Wyckoff Reformed Church
580 Wyckoff Avenue
in Wyckoff
MAP 9 › A3

In the town of Wyckoff is the **Van Voorhees-
Quackenbush-Zabriskie House,** built in 1824 in the
Federal style—although with a "Dutch" ownership
pedigree. It is operated as a municipal museum.
Nearby is the **Wyckoff Reformed Church,** built
around 1808 while Peter de Witt was pastor of the
local congregation.

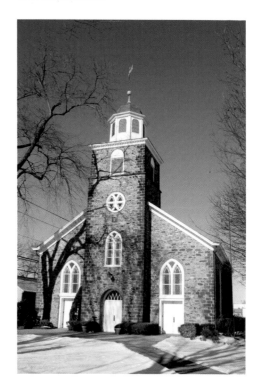

Passaic River Valley

Further to the south is the Passaic River valley (after which Passaic
County is named), another area with a strong Dutch-American
legacy. Wayne, in particular, has a valuable concentration of Dutch-
American houses.

Dey Mansion

The Georgian-style **Dey Mansion** was built between 1740 and 1750 by Dirck Dey, a Dutch-born planter. It was completed by his son Theunis, who commanded the Bergen County militia during the American Revolution. General Washington used the house as his headquarters in July, October, and November 1780. It is now a museum run by the Passaic County Parks Department. On the grounds are a blacksmith shop and formal gardens.

199 Totowa Road
in Wayne
MAP 9 › A4

Schuyler Colfax House

The **Schuyler Colfax House** is Wayne's oldest house and was built in 1695–1696 by pioneer settler Arent Schuyler (1662–1730). It remained in the Schuyler family for eight generations and is currently a small museum.

2343 Hamburg Turnpike
(U.S. 202) in Wayne
MAP 9 › A4

Dutch Houses in Wayne

The **Van Riper-Hopper House,** built in 1786 by Uriah Van Riper, is a typical example of Dutch-American architecture. Built of stone, it comprises five rooms on the first floor and four bedrooms upstairs and is well furnished with antiques. The Van Riper-Hopper House and the **Mead-Van Duyne House (right),** a brownstone Dutch-American farmhouse dating from 1706 and later moved to this area, together form a museum complex that is worth visiting.

533 Berdan Avenue
in Wayne
MAP 9 › A4

Hamilton-Van Wagoner House

The **Hamilton-Van Wagoner House** is another typical example of early Dutch-American architecture in the region, although it was built around 1816. It is now a small living-history museum, re-creating early-19th-century daily life.

971 Valley Road in Clifton
MAP 9 › C6

MAP 10

The Delaware Water Gap

Sussex and Warren Counties

ROUTE 6

I- 84

ROUTE 6

PENNSYLVANIA

Milford •

RT 206

ROUTE 209

CO RD 521

Westbrook-Bell House •

Dingman's Ferry •

CO RD 560

ROUTE 209

DELAWARE RIVER

Isaac Van Campen House •

• Wallpack Center

OLD MINE RD

ROUTE 615

DELAWARE

ROUTE 209

RT 606

• Millbrook

Abraham Van Campen House

Abraham Van
Campen Homestead

MILLBROOK RD

A

B

C

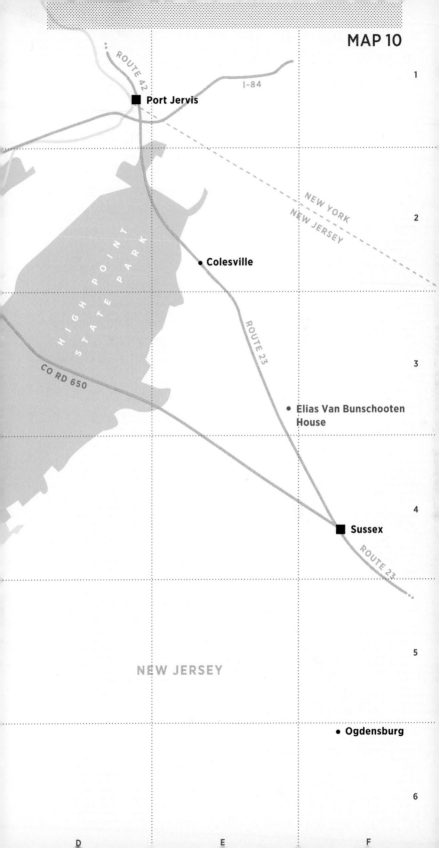

MAP 10

1

ROUTE 42

I-84

■ Port Jervis

2

NEW YORK
NEW JERSEY

● Colesville

ROUTE 23

3

CO RD 650

HIGH POINT STATE PARK

● Elias Van Bunschooten House

4

■ Sussex

ROUTE 23

5

NEW JERSEY

● Ogdensburg

6

D   E   F

The Delaware Water Gap

The beautiful and largely unspoiled Delaware Water Gap National Recreation Area along the Delaware River in northwestern New Jersey is in the area known in Dutch days as the Minisink region. This was the terminus of the Old Mine Road which, according to legend, was built by the Dutch from Esopus (today's Kingston in New York State) during the New Netherland period to access copper and gold mines. Historians and archaeologists, however, say that the road was built in the 18th century as a farm road running from Port Jervis through Ellenville and Hurley to Kingston, New York. There are still Dutch colonial farmhouses located along this scenic road, which today is known as County Road 606.

We suggest you start at the Delaware Water Gap crossing at Route 80 and travel north. From there, River Road heads north along the east embankment of the Delaware River and soon becomes County Road 606.

Abraham Van Campen Homestead and Farmhouse

Abraham Van Campen Homestead (below)
Millbrook Village
MAP 10 › A6

Abraham Van Campen Farmhouse and Barn
Millbrook Village
MAP 10 › B6

Gerrit Jansen van Campen was a soldier who came to New Netherland around 1659 and settled at Esopus. His grandson, Abraham Van Campen, is credited as the first and most prominent settler of an area formerly called Pahaquarry, north of the Delaware Water Gap. Abraham bought land ca. 1732 within a tract then named Pahaqualin. He also served as colonel of the West Jersey troops in the French and Indian War (1754–1763). He built the **Abraham Van Campen Homestead,** which served as the headquarters for early settlers in the Minisink Valley. A fort once stood nearby and housed a garrison of 250 men. Built of red sandstone with a stucco exterior finish, the house has very small windows typical of the early frontier residences. The structure, not currently inhabited, stands near the south

bank of Van Campen Brook on the east side of
the Old Mine Road and is easy to miss. Look for
it approximately nine miles to the north on the
right side of the main road, past the Coppermine
Inn and the Turtle Beach swimming beach.
Van Campen Brook was originally named Van
Campen's Mill Brook after the mill operated by the
Van Campen family.

   Located a few miles further north in Millbrook
Village, which was also named for the mill, is the
18th-century **Abraham Van Campen Farmhouse**,
moved to this re-created village in 1978 from
its original location two miles south. The **Van
Campen Barn**, located closer to the Old Mine
Road, built in the late 1800s, was also moved to
its current site from a location a quarter mile away.
Many of the structures here are maintained by the
Millbrook Village Society.

Isaac Van Campen House

Old Mine Road in
Walpack Township
MAP 10 › B4

The **Isaac Van Campen House** (also known as
the **Van Campen Inn**) was a former yaugh house
(mostly likely from the Dutch word *jacht*, meaning
hunting lodge) on a now-unpaved section of the
Old Mine Road in Walpack Township at the lower
end of Shapanack Flats, directly west and over the
ridge from Walpack Center. It was built ca. 1750
by Abraham's nephew Isaac. During the French
and Indian War, militia were assigned to a fort
north of the structure called "Headquarters," and
150 settlers sought protection here. In December
1776, General Horatio Gates and seven regiments
camped on the Shapanack Flats while marching
on the Old Mine Road from Kingston, New York,
to reinforce Washington's army in Trenton. The
building is open for tours offered by the Walpack
Historical Society. The three Van Campen sites are
managed by the U.S. Department of the Interior
as part of the Delaware Water Gap National
Recreation Area.

Dingmans Ferry Bridge

MAP 10 › C3

The **Dingmans Ferry Bridge**, further north along
the Delaware River, crosses into Pennsylvania. (It
may interest you to know that the "Pennsylvania
Dutch" were actually German immigrants.) It

is among the last privately owned toll bridges in the United States and is operated by a stockholding company, the Dingmans Choice and Delaware Bridge Company, whose members are descendants of early settlers. The first toll bridge at this site was built by a descendant of Andrew Dingman, a Dutch pioneer from Kinderhook, New York, who opened a ferry crossing here in 1735.

Westbrook-Bell House

North off the Old Mine Road, the privately owned **Westbrook-Bell House** in Sandyston Township may be the oldest structure in the region, probably dating from ca. 1725, and is designated by an historical marker. Unfortunately, it has not been inhabited in several years. At the time of this writing, plans to further develop the Delaware Water Gap National Recreation Area include demolishing some of the early settlers' legacy, but we hope not the Westbrook-Bell House.

Old Mine Road in Sandyston Township
MAP 10 › C3

Reverend Elias Van Bunschooten House

Along Route 23 North in Wantage Township, between the towns of Colesville and Sussex, you will find the **Reverend Elias Van Bunschooten House,** built in 1787. Van Bunschooten, an 18th-century Dutch Protestant minister, was well known in the region for his boundless energy and generosity. The Dutch colonial house is run as a small museum by the Daughters of the American Revolution.

1097 Route 23 in Wantage Township
MAP 10 › E3

American-Dutch Antiques

Roderic Blackburn

When the Dutch arrived in New Netherland, they began making the tools and furnishings needed to supplement the few brought or imported from the Dutch Republic. Not many artifacts from the old country survive today. An exception is the quintessential Dutch piece of furniture, the "kas," or cupboard. Actually a large wardrobe, the kas (*kast* in Dutch) was the Dutch closet for storage of valuables, especially textiles, which, unlike today, were expensive. The American-made version was simpler, usually of gumwood tree rather than expensive tropical woods.

Of 17th-century furnishings made here, few have survived—and silver comprises the majority of the surviving examples. For instance, the Brandywine bowl and cast-handle spoon, associated with long-lasting Dutch social traditions, continued to be made by New York silversmiths, often of Dutch descent (such as Cornelis Kierstede, Peter Van Dyck, Adriaen Bancker, Benjamin Wynkoop, Nicholas Roosevelt, and Tobias Stoutenburgh) and used well into the 18th century.

The Dutch also imported utilitarian earthenware and decorative Delftware. Since it was rarely used, Delftware survives in greater quantity than earthenware, which, when eventually broken in use, was dumped down the outhouse hole, only to be avidly excavated and reconstituted by modern archaeologists and pot hunters.

In addition to Bibles, church and domestic silver, other objects in the Dutch style have survived in relatively large numbers. Tin (such as plates), pewter, brass, and copper objects (tobacco boxes, candlesticks) may still be found in public and private collections and in antique shops. As early as the 1680s, the Anglo-Dutch began to adopt English fashions in applied arts while conservative Dutch, especially those living farthest from New York City, continued to prefer furnishings in the Dutch style. The kas was made well into the 19th century. Versions of Dutch-style slat-back chairs were still being made in New Jersey in the 1850s. One of the most

ABOVE: American kas from the Bevier House Museum
LEFT: 17th-century *kast* from the Dutch Republic

Seal of Petrus Stuyvesant

common New York chairs, the fiddle-back, long popular with
people of Dutch descent, is actually an English form adopted in the
1750s. Yet some true Dutch artifacts may be traced way back, like
the medial-stretcher table whose simple structural system dates to
Medieval times; the spoon rack, so closely associated with Bergen
County, New Jersey; the carved foot warmer and the draw-bar
table whose leaves are held up by simple, extended wood draw-
bars rather than gate legs.

Hundreds of early portraits of Dutch family members, often
rather crudely painted in the English manner, survive (mostly
in museums), as do dozens of paintings based on Dutch Bible

Silver tankard, ca. 1700, with the
Van Cortlandt coat of arms, by
Cornelius Kierstede

engravings. Other non-household objects, like farm equipment,
continued to be made in the Dutch tradition. New Netherland was
a wheat-growing colony and the Dutch type of scythe, with its arm
brace and associated mat hook, continued in use for a long time.
For hunting the Dutch preferred their own style of flintlock gun
called the Dutch long fowler. Multipurpose (it was used to hunt
water fowl, deer, and even Indians), its especially long barrel gave
its shot higher velocity.

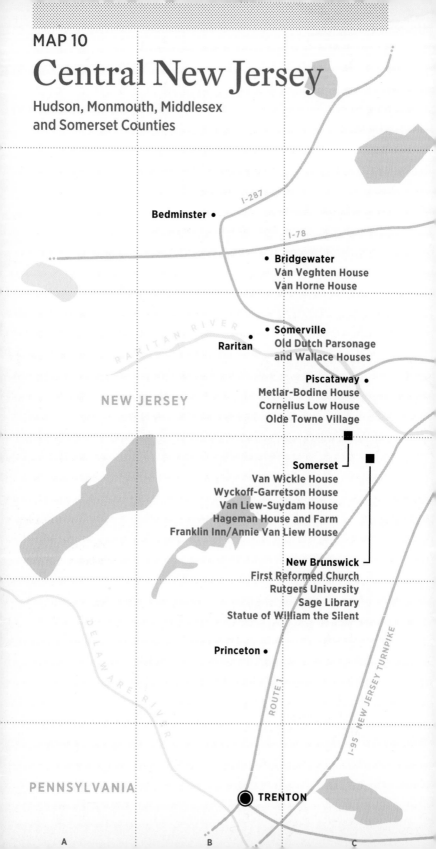

MAP 10

Central New Jersey

Hudson, Monmouth, Middlesex
and Somerset Counties

I-287

I-78

Bedminster •

• **Bridgewater**
Van Veghten House
Van Horne House

RARITAN RIVER

•
Raritan

• **Somerville**
Old Dutch Parsonage
and Wallace Houses

NEW JERSEY

Piscataway •
Metlar-Bodine House
Cornelius Low House
Olde Towne Village

■

Somerset
Van Wickle House
Wyckoff-Garretson House
Van Liew-Suydam House
Hageman House and Farm
Franklin Inn/Annie Van Liew House

■

New Brunswick
First Reformed Church
Rutgers University
Sage Library
Statue of William the Silent

DELAWARE RIVER

Princeton •

ROUTE 1

NEW JERSEY TURNPIKE

I-95

PENNSYLVANIA

◉ **TRENTON**

A   B   C

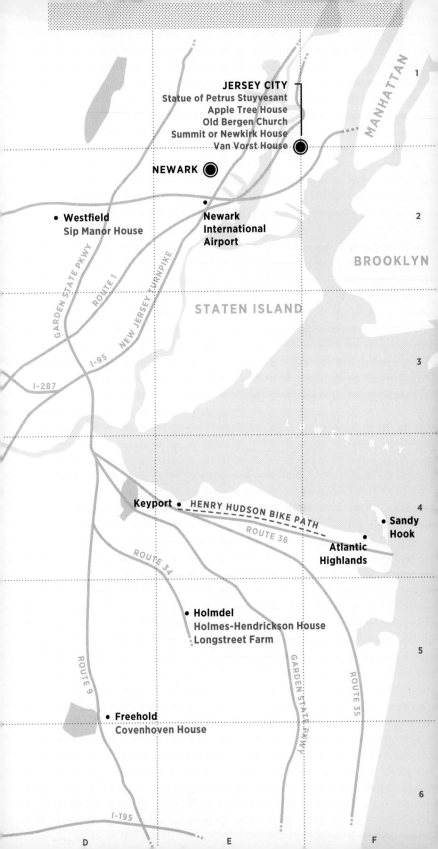

Central New Jersey

Jersey City

Jersey City is located on the New Jersey side of the Holland Tunnel. Contrary to popular misconception, the tunnel is not named after the Dutch but in honor of Clifford Milburn Holland, who was the chief engineer on the project. Jersey City is the location of two once-important New Netherland sites: the patroonship of Pavonia and the village of Bergen, a small settlement surrounded by a stockade that can still be traced in the street plan around the crossing of Bergen Avenue and Academy Street.

Although the entire area encompassing present-day Jersey City was originally included in the patroonship of Pavonia, the name now tends to be associated with the downtown Jersey City area. The patroonship of Pavonia was initially established in 1630 by Michiel Pauw, a director of the Dutch West India Company (WIC). Pauw sent Cornelis van Vorst to be his agent at the patroonship but soon sold it back to the WIC. The patroonship was strategically located at a site that Native Americans could easily reach to trade. WIC director Willem Kieft and his council resolved in 1639 that the local Native Americans should contribute to the building of fortifications and the upkeep of soldiers and sailors. That demand, and the refusal of Indian groups to pay, strained the already deteriorating relations. Hostilities occurred throughout 1642, and in February 1643, when a group of Indians sought refuge in Pavonia from an attack by Mahicans, a company of soldiers and colonists crossed the river to attack them. In what has become known as the Pavonia Massacre, 80 Native-American men, women, and children were killed. The incident contributed to the recalling of Kieft by the WIC directors.

Statue of Petrus Stuyvesant

Jersey City itself has a few modest relics from the
Dutch period. The **statue of Petrus Stuyvesant**
stood outside of what is today the Martin
Luther King Jr. School, located at the heart of
the former village of Bergen. It was erected in
1910 to commemorate the 250th anniversary of
Stuyvesant's charter of the village in 1661. At the
time of writing, the statue is being restored and
has been temporarily removed.

886 Bergen Avenue
in Jersey City
MAP 11 › E2

Apple Tree House

Close to the former site of the Stuyvesant statue
stands the **Apple Tree House** or **Van Wagenen
House,** possibly built ca. 1658. One of the oldest
houses in the city, the site has been closed for
restoration for several years. According to a
local legend, in 1779 George Washington and
the Marquis de Lafayette met to discuss strategy
under an apple tree in its garden.

298 Academy Street
in Jersey City
MAP 11 › E2

Sip Manor House

5 Cherry Lane in Westfield
MAP 11 › D2

Until the 1920s one of New Jersey's oldest houses,
Sip Manor House, which dates from 1664–1666,
stood nearby on the corner of Newkirk Street
and Bergen Avenue. It still exists as a private
residence, but has been moved to Westfield.

Old Bergen Church

1 Highland Avenue
in Jersey City
MAP 11 › E2

The Greek Revival **Old Bergen (Dutch Reformed)
Church,** was built in 1841, as the inscription (in
Dutch) on a stone above the entrance attests.
The **cemetery** across from the church (entrance
on Bergen Street) still has a number of Dutch-
inscribed stones.

Summit or Newkirk House

510 Summit Avenue
in Jersey City
MAP 11 › E2

The **Summit** or **Newkirk House** probably
dates its core to 1690, although the building,
now a restaurant, underwent many alterations
in later periods.

Henry Hudson Bust

Further north, in an area of the city called the
Heights (once Hudson City), you will find a
gilded **bust of Henry Hudson** in Riverview-Fiske
Park, which overlooks the Hudson Valley towards
Manhattan. Try to find Holland Street (not
signed), which runs just north of the park down
towards Paterson Plank Road. It is one of the
last cobblestone streets in Jersey City. Nearby
stands the privately owned **Van Vorst House,**
built ca. 1740.

Riverview-Fiske Park
on Bowers Street
in the Heights
MAP 11 › E2

Van Vorst House
531 Palisade Avenue
in Heights
MAP 11 › E2

 From Jersey City take the New Jersey Turnpike south to Exit 11
and exit at Route 9 South. After crossing the Raritan River, turn
on Route 35 East to continue the tour.

Henry Hudson Trail

The northern section of the **Henry Hudson Trail**
runs along the southern bank of Raritan Bay,
parallel to Route 35. (Note: the trail has some
missing links.) The trail was created by the
Monmouth County Park System in the National
Rails-to-Trails Network, which converts railroad
rights-of-way into scenic trails (with a right of
reversal back to rail). The **scenic lookout at Mount
Mitchell** in Atlantic Highlands, the end of the trail,
is the best place to get a view of Sandy Hook and
the Raritan Bay, with Staten Island and Manhattan
in the distance. In a residential neighborhood in
Atlantic Highlands it is possible, though difficult, to
find the **Henry Hudson Springs historical plaque**
(on Bayside Drive near Prospect Road) that marks
the spot where Henry Hudson reportedly drew
water when he visited Raritan Bay in 1609. Take
Prospect Road north off of Ocean Boulevard and
head down the steep drive towards the ocean. A
small wooden sign on a brick wall marks the old
stone steps that lead down to the marker. (The
steps can be slippery: use caution.)

Scenic Lookout
Mount Mitchell in
Atlantic Highlands
MAP 11 › E4

**Henry Hudson Springs
Historical Plaque**
Bayside Drive near
Prospect Road
MAP 11 › E4

Holmes-Hendrickson House

63 Longstreet Road
in Holmdel
MAP 11 › E5

Slightly south of the trail, the **Holmes-Hendrickson House** was moved from a nearby site. This wood-framed house was built by William Holmes, who was of Dutch and English ancestry, in the tradition similar to Dutch farmhouses on Long Island. In 1756 Holmes sold the house to his cousin Garret Hendrickson, the grandson of Daniel Hendrickson, who migrated to Monmouth County from Flatbush around 1693. The house has a Dutch floor plan with two large rooms in the front, two smaller rooms in the back, and a kitchen wing on the side. However, the framing of the house has more similarities to the English houses in Connecticut than the H-bent framing of Dutch houses.

Longstreet Farm

50 Longstreet Road
in Holmdel
MAP 11 › E5

Close to the Holmes-Hendrickson House stands the **Longstreet Farm**, which includes a Dutch barn on its grounds. It was once owned by descendants of Dirck Stoffelszen Langestraat (who Americanized the family name to "Longstreet").

Covenhoven House

Further south is the **Covenhoven House** that
is maintained as a museum by the Monmouth
County Historical Association. It was built ca. 1752–
1753 by a successful Dutch farmer named William
A. Covenhoven, son of Albert Couvenhoven (the
name was changed by the next generation), who
moved from Flatlands, Brooklyn, to Monmouth
County prior to 1709. Although William and his
wife, Elizabeth Van Cleef, were Dutch Americans,
their house was built in the English Georgian
style. As such, it is an example of how some
Dutch-American families adapted to the dominant
English culture of colonial New Jersey. It not
only hosts a nice cupboard, or kas, painted *en
grisaille* (in shades of grey), but also has elegantly
painted paneling in the bedroom upstairs, which
includes a battle scene between Dutch and
English warships. The house was occupied by the
British general Henry Clinton prior to the Battle of
Monmouth in the summer of 1778.

150 West Main Street
in Freehold
MAP 11 › D5

Middlesex and Somerset Counties

Two of America's oldest counties, Middlesex and Somerset, named after English counties, were chartered in the 1680s. Most of their early residents were Dutch, and both counties retain evidence of their Dutch heritage, particularly along the Raritan River.

 We suggest you start a tour of Middlesex and Somerset Counties in New Brunswick.

First Reformed Church

9 Bayard Street
in New Brunswick
MAP 11 › C4

The earliest congregation of the **First Reformed Church** in New Brunswick was organized in 1717 by Dutch settlers from Brooklyn at what was then known as Indian's Ferry along the Raritan River. There were three structures before the current First Reformed Church. The first was a wood building known as "the church at three miles run," located on the corner of Burnet and Schureman Streets. (Schureman Street was named after James Schureman, 1756–1824, who was a delegate to the Continental Congress, a United States senator and congressman, and mayor of New Brunswick.) It was here that the Reverend Theodorus Jacobus Frelinghuysen (1691–1747) and the pastor Gilbert Tennent (1703–1764) of the First Presbyterian Church in New Brunswick became leaders of the "Great Awakening," a religious revival movement in the 18th century that had a profound impact on colonial America's religious landscape and that split many congregations. The second church was a square, stone structure erected in 1765 at the present location. During the American Revolution it was occupied by the British and converted into a hospital and later a stable. In 1799 a congregant named Sarah Van Doren and other women started a Sunday school, which is considered the oldest continuously operating Sunday school in the United States. The present-day church was constructed in 1811–1812.

Rutgers University

Rutgers University was originally chartered in 1766 as Queens College by New Jersey governor William Franklin. In the 19th century it was renamed after Colonel Henry Rutgers (1745–1830), a Revolutionary War veteran and a well-regarded member of the Dutch Reformed Church. The college's original mission was the training of Dutch Reformed ministers (*domines*) in America. It grew out of a schism in the church between the Coetus faction, which advocated an American-trained ministry, and the Conferentie faction, which insisted that all Dutch Reformed ministers be ordained in Amsterdam.

536 George Street
in New Brunswick
MAP 11 › C4

Sage Library at the New Brunswick Theological Seminary

The college's first president was Reverend Jacob Hardenbergh (1736–1790) of Somerset, New Jersey, who became an active supporter of the American Revolution. Rutgers' main administration building is named Old Queens: the cornerstone was laid in 1809 to house Queens College, the Reformed Dutch seminary known as "the Professorate," and a preparatory school. The **Sage Library at the New Brunswick Theological**

21 Seminary Place
in New Brunswick
MAP 11 › C4

Seminary contains Dutch-language bibles and the archives of the Reformed Church in America.

Statue of William the Silent

Between Old Queens
and the New Brunswick
Theological Seminary
in New Brunswick
MAP 11 › C4

Located between Old Queens and the New Brunswick Theological Seminary is a **statue of William the Silent** (1533–1584), Count of Nassau, Prince of Orange, who was the leader of the revolution against Spain that resulted in the Dutch Republic. The statue was erected by the Holland Society in 1928. Dutch New Jerseyans maintain their interest in genealogy as active members of the Genealogical and Biographical Society and the Holland Society of New York.

The Enslaved Africans and the Native Americans

Jaap Jacobs

Jan Rodrigues (probably a Dutch spelling of Juan Rodriquez), a "mulatto born in St Domingo" claiming to be "a free man," was very likely the first black person in New Netherland. He is reported as sailing in 1613 with Captain Mossel on the *Jonge Tobias*. Having received his wages and some tools, he spent the subsequent winter somewhere along the Hudson River, possibly on Manhattan Island, where he conducted trade with the Indians. We know little more about him except that the next spring he became involved in a row about fur trading between two Dutch trading groups.

Within a few years after the Dutch settled on Manhattan, the first enslaved Africans arrived. It is likely that they were captured on Spanish and Portuguese ships in the Caribbean, as the import of slaves in New Netherland directly from Africa only started in the 1650s. The economy of New Netherland was not based on plantations, and thus the number of enslaved Africans remained relatively low: in 1639 approximately 100 slaves served the West India Company (WIC) and private owners. This number rose to about 150 in 1655; by this time a small number of slaves had been set free. The arrival of 291 slaves just prior to the English takeover in 1664 increased the number to approximately 500–550. Africans, both free and enslaved, made up around 6–8% of the New Netherland population, with a concentration in New Amsterdam.

Initially, all enslaved Africans were owned by the WIC and were put to work on various projects that required manual labor. Although the prices paid for enslaved people in New Netherland lagged behind those in the Dutch colony of Curaçao, only the wealthy could afford to purchase them. In 1665 the number of slaveholders was still quite low—12% of the 254 persons taxed that year. After 1674 ownership gradually became more general, and by 1703 no less than 41% of the households in New York City owned slaves. In the New Netherland decades, some African slaves were able to hold property, provide testimony in court, and

ON BOARD A SLAVE-SHIP.

purchase their freedom. North of New Amsterdam, a number of free Africans lived together on their own land and formed a small village. In the 18th century the slave regime in New York became much harsher than in the previous century. By then, many farmers of Dutch origin possessed one or more slave laborers, and their descendants were often prominent opponents of the abolition of slavery in New York State.

Unlike enslaved Africans, Native Americans did not become part of colonial society, although trade contacts with Native Americans were of paramount importance to New Netherland in the early decades. Groups belonging to the Iroquois Confederacy in the hinterland were the main suppliers of furs. For trade transactions, shell money (called *sewant* by the Dutch colonists and *wampum* by the English, using different Algonquin words) was indispensable. As silver money was rare in the colony, shell beads and peltries were used instead, representing set rates. The value of the fur trade made Dutch officials careful in their dealings with the powerful Iroquois, but the groups along the coast and the Hudson River (Delawares or Lenapes, Munsees, and Mahicans) did not have a similar importance for trade. Their decreasing trade significance to the Dutch, who coveted the fertile flood plains along the Hudson River, led to three Munsee wars: Kieft's

Not-to-way, a Chief, by George Catlin. Not-a-way was an Iroquois, one of the most powerful Native American groups in the Northeast.

War in the 1640s, the "Peach War" (a term coined by Washington Irving) in 1655, and the conflict with the Esopus Indians in the 1660s. Atrocities were committed by both sides, but the Native Americans, already weakened by unfamiliar European diseases, suffered most. Dutch tactics of destroying supplies, such as maize pits, resulted in famine and forced the Native Americans to agree to Dutch peace terms and to vacate lands that the colonists subsequently put to their own agricultural use.

Even so, land acquisition by conquest was relatively rare. In many cases, land changed hands through purchase. As Native Americans conceived of land property in quite a different way from Europeans, land purchases resulted in many misunderstandings. Native Americans often reoccupied land vacated by colonists, who then had to purchase the land again—two more times in the case of Staten Island. In contrast, Manhattan Island, which was famously purchased by Pieter Minuit in 1626, remained in Dutch hands until New Netherland was taken over by the English in 1664.

Metlar-Bodine House

1281 River Road
in Piscataway
MAP 11 › C3

There is extensive evidence of Dutch heritage along the Raritan River. In the 1730s Peter Bodine settled in the place known as Raritan Landing located at the head of navigation on the north side of the Raritan River and built the **Metlar-Bodine House.** From this location it was necessary to transship goods by the road that ran along the north side of the river to the interior reaches of the Raritan and Millstone Rivers. Peter Bodine and his son John built warehouses along the flats and established trade with country stores in Bound Brook and South Branch, Dutch farmers in the outlying areas, and later with nearby copper mines. Soon a small community of Dutch and English merchants developed at Raritan Landing. During the American Revolution, Raritan Landing was a major strategic location because it had the only bridge across the Raritan River, built in 1772. The British established an encampment there during the winter of 1776–1777. At its height, Raritan Landing had about 100 inhabitants and 70 buildings. However, the landing began to decline in the early 19th century, displaced first by steamboats that could only navigate as far as the nearby town of New Brunswick, then by the Delaware and Raritan Canal, and finally by the railroad built through New Brunswick. The Metlar-Bodine House was seriously damaged in a fire in 2003, but is now under restoration.

Cornelius Low House

One of the Dutch merchants at Raritan Landing, Adolphus Hardenbrook from New York City, had many connections with merchants there. He attracted several of them, including Abraham Van Ranst and Evert Duyckinck, to move to Raritan Landing. Other Dutch merchants, Peter Low and his brother Cornelius, also moved to Raritan Landing. In 1741 Cornelius Low built an English Georgian-style mansion, the **Cornelius Low House,** on the bluff overlooking Raritan Landing. Today it is a small museum of medical science run by the Middlesex County Cultural and Heritage Commission. Many of the upper-class Dutch merchants of New York adopted English culture and even joined the Anglican Church. Thus, it is fitting that Cornelius Low (1699/1700–1777), with his commercial contacts in New York, lived in an English-style house. (Low was also a Loyalist during the American Revolution.) The house includes some attractive fireplaces with Dutch tiles and a beautiful staircase.

1225 River Road in Piscataway
MAP 11 › C3

Olde Towne Village

1050 River Road
in Piscataway
MAP 11 › C3

Located a short distance west of Raritan Landing is the charming re-created **East Jersey Olde Towne Village,** which comprises buildings that were moved to this location and others that were completely reconstructed. Of particular interest to those who want to learn more about Dutch history is the re-creation of the original **Church at Three-Mile Run (left)** and the restored **Jacobus Vanderveer House (below),** dating from the 1760s, which was originally located in Pluckemin in Somerset County. Jacobus Vanderveer moved from Flatbush to the North Branch of the Raritan River around 1745. Much of the original fabric of the house remains intact, including wood paneling above the fireplace and original pine-board flooring. During the American Revolution, General Henry Knox used the house as his headquarters, while the Continental Army camped at Pluckemin (Plukemin) in the winter of 1778–1779. A renovated Dutch barn may also be found in the village. The Middlesex County Cultural and Heritage Commission manages the village of Olde Towne and runs interpretive programs there.

Van Wickle House

There is more to see in the Raritan Valley. Approximately 800 acres in the valley were originally purchased by Evert Van Wickle of New Amersfoort, Long Island. In 1722 Evert's son Simon and his new wife, Gerardina Couwenhoven (1705–1754), built a wood-frame farmhouse, the **Van Wickle House.** Unlike the farmhouses built by other Dutch families along River Road in Piscataway, which are oriented with their gable ends toward the road, the Van Wickle House faces the river. At this location the Old Middlebush Road (today DeMott Lane) linked the settlement of Middlebush with the Raritan River. Today the house is a museum run by the Meadows Foundation. Among the events it sponsors is a Dutch St. Nicholas Day celebration in early December.

1289 Easton Avenue in Somerset

MAP 11 › C4

Dutch Houses in Somerset

Wyckoff-Garretson
House (above)
215 South Middlebush
Road in Somerset
MAP 11 › C4

Van Liew-Suydam House
280 South Middlebush
Road in Somerset
MAP 11 › C4

Hageman House
and Farm
209 South Middlebush
Road in Somerset
MAP 11 › C4

Franklin Inn/Annie Van
Liew House
2371 Amwell Road
in Somerset
MAP 11 › C4

Further inland from the Raritan River is the
Wyckoff-Garretson House, also managed by the
Meadows Foundation. The founder of the Wyckoff
family was Pieter Claesen Wyckoff (1625–1694),
who built the well-known Wyckoff Farmhouse in
Brooklyn. Pieter's son Cornelis Wyckoff (b. 1656)
purchased 1,200 acres of land along the Raritan
River in 1701 and parceled them out to his four
sons. One of his sons, John Wyckoff, built the
oldest part of this house around 1730, employing
Dutch craftsmen from Brooklyn. The house was
enlarged in 1805 by another Dutch farmer, Samuel
Garretson from Hillsborough.

Other houses in the Somerset area with
some Dutch ancestry, although of 19th-century
character, are the 1875 **Van Liew-Suydam House,**
the mid-19th-century **Hageman House and
Farm,** as well as the ca. 1752 **Franklin Inn/Annie
Van Liew House.** All three buildings are open by
appointment and run by the Meadows Foundation.

Old Dutch Parsonage and Wallace Houses

The **Old Dutch Parsonage House** was built in
1751. It was the residence of Reverend John
Frelinghuysen (1727–1754), the son of Reverend
Theodorus Jacobus Frelinghuysen. In 1758
it became the home of the Reverend Jacob
Hardenbergh, who in 1766 was one of the
founders and the first president of Queens
College (later Rutgers University). Reverend
Hardenbergh was an active supporter of the
American Revolution and a delegate to the New
Jersey Provincial Congress. In 1913 the house was
moved from its original location to the property of
the adjacent **Wallace House** and is maintained by
the New Jersey Division of Parks and Recreation
as a state historic site, although at this writing it is
in poor condition.

**Old Dutch Parsonage
House (below)**
38 Washington Place
in Somerville
MAP 11 › B3

Wallace House
65 Washington Place
in Somerville
MAP 11 › B3

Dutch Houses in Bridgewater

In Bridgewater you will find the 18th-century
Van Horne House, as well as the **Van Veghten
House,** the current home of the Somerset County
Historical Society; both sites are open to the
public. The Van Veghten House was built in the
late-17th century by Michael Van Veghten and still
stands in its original location on the north bank of
the Raritan River.

Van Horne House
941 Main Street
MAP 11 › B2

Van Veghten House
9 Van Veghten Drive
MAP 11 › B2

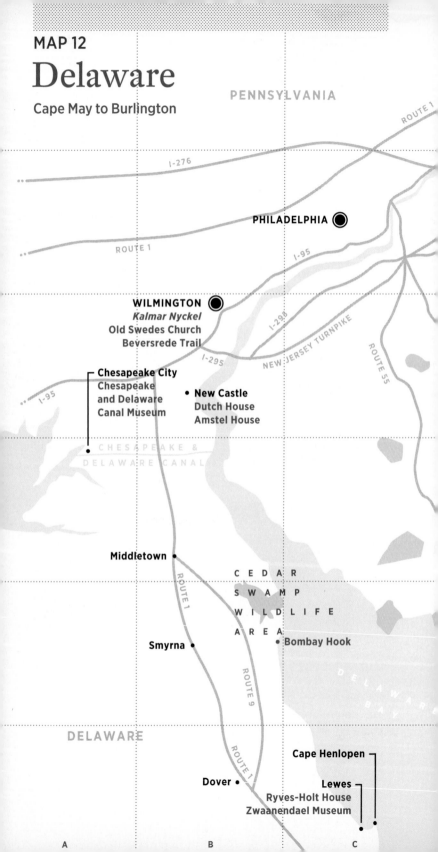

MAP 12
Delaware
Cape May to Burlington

PENNSYLVANIA

ROUTE 1

I-276

ROUTE 1

PHILADELPHIA ◉

I-95

I-296

WILMINGTON ◉
Kalmar Nyckel
**Old Swedes Church
Beversrede Trail**

NEW JERSEY TURNPIKE

I-295

ROUTE 55

**Chesapeake City
Chesapeake
and Delaware
Canal Museum**

I-95

• **New Castle
Dutch House
Amstel House**

C H E S A P E A K E &
D E L A W A R E   C A N A L

Middletown •

C E D A R

S W A M P

W I L D L I F E

A R E A

ROUTE 1

Smyrna •

• **Bombay Hook**

D E L A W A R E   B A Y

ROUTE 9

DELAWARE

ROUTE 1

Cape Henlopen

Dover •

Lewes
**Ryves-Holt House
Zwaanendael Museum**

A   B   C

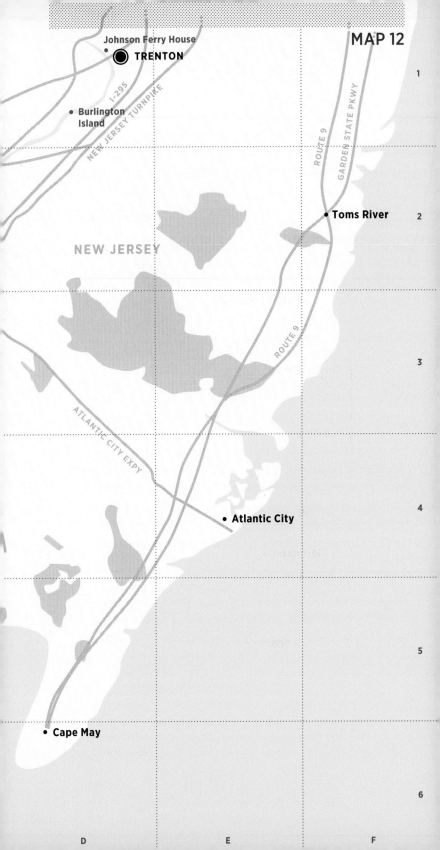

MAP 12

Johnson Ferry House
● TRENTON

I-295

NEW JERSEY TURNPIKE

● Burlington
Island

ROUTE 9

GARDEN STATE PKWY

1

2

● Toms River

NEW JERSEY

ROUTE 9

3

ATLANTIC CITY EXPY

4

● Atlantic City

5

● Cape May

6

D   E   F

Delaware

For the Dutch colony of New Netherland, the Delaware River was of major geopolitical importance. In the hands of the English, it would have posed a threat to the Dutch fur-trading operations far to the north at Fort Orange (Albany). Fortunately, the English were not aware of its potential. Back in 1609, Henry Hudson had stuck his nose into Delaware Bay on his way to Manhattan, only to conclude that it wasn't a passage to the riches of the Far East but merely the mouth of a river. In the southernmost area you will still find Dutch geographical terms such as "kill" (from the Dutch word *kille*, meaning body of water) and "hook" *(*from the Dutch word *hoeck,* meaning point). Although very little is left of the Dutch presence in this area, this tour will take you through an attractive landscape that includes the last remnants of Dutch settlement.

Cape May

Modern explorers of the Delaware River should begin, as Henry Hudson did, by experiencing the expanse of the bay. A good place to start is Cape May at the tip of New Jersey, named after Dutch captain Cornelis May of Hoorn, who arrived here in 1613. It is now a popular summer resort and birding destination, featuring a large collection of Victorian homes. Nearby is a car ferry that will take you to the charming town of Lewes, Delaware. Just before landing, you will pass Cape Henlopen, named after Dutch merchant Thijmen Jacobsz Hinlopen (1572–1637) who was involved in the early New Netherland trade. If you take the 90-minute trip, you will understand its attraction for the early explorers of the 17th century (and for whales).

Zwaanendael Museum

102 King's Highway at Savannah Road in Lewes
MAP 12 › C6

The Dutch first settled Lewes in 1631 as a patroonship conceived and financed by David Pietersz de Vries (1593–1655), Samuel Blommaert (1583–1651), and other investors. They aimed to establish a train-oil factory to profit from the seasonal appearance of whales in the bay.

Twenty-eight men settled on the site, where they built a small fort named Swanendael. The 300th anniversary of that settlement was commemorated by the opening in 1931 of the **Zwaanendael Museum,** modeled after the town hall of Hoorn. (De Vries was from Hoorn.) The museum is a showcase for the maritime, military, and social history of the area and its Dutch roots. Although a stream nearby was traditionally called *Hoeren Kill* (Whore Kill, later Harlots Creek, now Lewes Creek) on old maps, that name actually had a less racy root than its translation suggests: the town of Hoorn.

Unfortunately, a disagreement with the local Indians led to the deaths of the early settlers in 1632. In 1663 this area became home to a group of Mennonites, Christian Anabaptists named after the Protestant reformer and Frisian (from the area of Friesland) Menno Simons, under the leadership of Pieter Cornelisz Plockhoy (ca. 1620–1664). The early settlement was destroyed a year later during the English takeover of New Netherland.

Ryves-Holt House

The oldest residence in Delaware, the **Ryves-Holt House,** dates from 1665 and houses the Lewes Historical Society. East of the center of town, on Pilottown Road across from a cemetery on a hill, stands a small **monument** dedicated to the first Dutch settlement. Limited archaeology nearby revealed evidence of wooden poles, which may have been part of the original palisade.

110 Shipcarpenter Street in Lewes
MAP 12 › C6

Bombay Hook National Wildlife Refuge

2591 Whitehall Neck Road
in Smyrna
MAP 12 › B5

Traveling north from Lewes along the Delaware coastal road, you should not miss the **Bombay Hook National Wildlife Refuge,** a large and mostly pristine wetland area known for its waterfowl and other migrating birds. Its name is an English attempt at the Dutch *Boomties Hoeck* (Little Grove of Trees Point), which served as a navigational marker for ships sailing up the Delaware River from the Delaware Bay.

Chesapeake and Delaware Canal Museum

815 Bethel Road in
Chesapeake City, Maryland
MAP 12 › A4

Further north along the river, you will cross a canal that is worthy of note. In 1659 Augustin Herrman (Augustijn Heermans) was commissioned by the WIC to investigate Maryland's claim to the Delaware region. While on his way overland to St. Mary's City (the capital of Lord Baltimore's colony), Herrman climbed a hill from which he could see waterways flowing on one side to the Delaware River and, on the other side, to the Chesapeake Bay. He noted in his journal that it would be possible to connect the two waterways with a canal, considerably reducing travel from the river to the bay. However, his vision didn't become a reality until 1829. At the south end of the canal in Chesapeake City, Maryland, you will find a portrait of Herrman hanging over the entrance door of the **Chesapeake and Delaware Canal Museum,** operated by the United States Army Corps of Engineers.

Dutch Words in American English

Nicoline van der Sijs

Until well into the 18th century, Dutch colonists formed a majority in parts of New York and New Jersey, where the Dutch language, often called "Low Dutch" by English colonists, remained common. As late as 1776 a sheriff had difficulty finding enough English speakers to organize a jury in this region. Not only descendants of Dutch colonists spoke Dutch, but also new speakers of the language, such as French, English, and German colonists. In addition, many slaves in the 18th century learned Dutch from their masters. For instance, the abolitionist and former slave, Sojourner Truth, born in 1797 on the estate of Colonel Johannes Hardenbergh in Swartekill in Ulster County, New York, spoke only Dutch until she was sold to an English family at the age of nine. Newspapers regularly carried advertisements offering Africans as slaves with the recommendation that they knew Dutch. The Dutch Reformed Church also stimulated the use of the Dutch language.

Seventeenth-century Dutch settlers and their descendants became part of the local elite, whose language had great prestige. Only after American independence in 1776 did the number of Dutch-speaking Americans rapidly decrease. In rural parts of New Jersey and the Mohawk Valley regional variants of the Dutch language persisted in the form of dialects called Jersey Dutch and Mohawk Dutch. These deviated considerably from Dutch as spoken in the Dutch Republic, as Dutch visitors remarked. The introduction of standardized education in 1910 eliminated the last remains of the Dutch language as it was spoken by the 17th-century colonists.

While many Dutch speakers gradually switched over to English, they retained several Dutch words. Some of these eventually became part of American English. What kind of words did the Americans borrow from Dutch? Somewhat surprisingly, a lot of Dutch words in American English appear in the culinary field. Names of pastries, sweets, and dainties were Anglicized, such as "cruller" and "waffle." The verb *snoepen* ("to eat sweets—on the sly") was borrowed as "to snoop," although the word in American English acquired the meaning "to go about in a sneaking way, to pry into." Popular loanwords from Dutch are "brandy" (from *brandewijn*) and "dope," which was originally borrowed from *dopen* in the sense of "dipping into sauce, gravy." It obviously has undergone a drastic change of meaning!

Many plant and animal names have also been borrowed from the Dutch language, as the Dutch were the first to provide many American flora and fauna with names. Americans therefore called corn salad "fetticus" (a corruption of the Dutch dialect name *vettekost*), supplied fish species with the names "killifish," "weakfish," "sea bass," and "spearing" (after Dutch *kilvis, weekvis, zeebaars,* and *spiering*) and called the wood marmot *aardvarken*, which was subsequently translated into American English as "groundhog." The Dutch also introduced "pit" for the hard seed of a fruit, or "stone" in British English.

Various terms for household goods, housing conditions, and utensils were borrowed from Dutch, such as "block," "boodle," "bake-oven," "bake-pan," "bed-pan," "blickey," "bockey," "dobber," "fyke" (net) and—probably the best-known—"stoop." The most important linguistic contribution in the field of trade and commerce was probably the ending "-ery" for words meaning "place where the activity mentioned by the verb is professionally executed": bakery, brewery, book bindery, and the Bowery (from *bouwerij,* a cultivated place or farm). Waterborne transport provided the originally Dutch terms "hooker," "keel" (boat), "pinkie," and "scow," while winter activities provided the loanwords "skate" and "sleigh." Borrowed names for children's games include "hoople" and "hunk," from which "hunky-dory" is derived.

Only a few generic concepts were borrowed. It has been suggested that the Dutch personal name *Jan-Kees* was the root for the general term for an inhabitant of the United States, a "Yankee," although this is unlikely. Americans also preferred the term "boss" (from *baas*) to the English "master." And what is more telling than the debt the American currency's universally recognized "dollar" owes to the Dutch word *daalder*!

New Castle

Following the Delaware River northward, you will eventually arrive at
the historic town of New Castle, which was laid out by Director General
Petrus Stuyvesant in 1651. The circumstances of its founding involved
a tale of Dutch-Swedish one-upmanship. In 1638 the New Sweden
Company established Fort Christina (named after the Swedish queen)
and a trading post at the site of present-day Wilmington, Delaware,
under the direction of Pieter Minuit (born ca. 1594). Minuit was a
former director of New Netherland and would later work for Sweden to
establish a settlement called New Sweden on the Delaware River, much
to the consternation of Stuyvesant and the WIC. Instead of resorting
to direct military action against this Swedish settlement, Stuyvesant
started a political game of chess. Under military cover he removed the
ordnance from Fort Nassau and crossed the river to Sand Hoeck where
he built a new trading post, Fort Casimir. The surrounding settlement
of New Amstel was subsequently laid out in a grid system, which has
survived in the center of today's town of New Castle.

Not only were the Dutch now on the west bank of the river, but they
were also present south of the Swedes, from where they could monitor
and harass Swedish vessels. The Swedes responded by building
another fort, Fort Nya Elfsborgh, farther south on the east bank near
present-day Salem, New Jersey. (There is a nuclear power plant on
the site today, close to the Fort Elfsborg-Salem Road.) The soldiers
stationed there tellingly referred to it as "Fort Myggenborg" or "Fort
Mosquito." (Not only was it an unpopular post, but it turned out to be
relatively ineffective as a defense post and did not play a significant
role in the Swedish-Dutch conflict over the area.)

The Dutch House,
New Castle

Dutch House and Amstel House

Dutch House
32 East 3rd Street
in New Castle
MAP 12 › B3

Amstel House (below)
2 East Fourth Street
in New Castle
MAP 12 › B3

New Castle itself still features two houses with modest Dutch links: the so-called **Dutch House,** which traces its origins to the 17th century and has some interesting Dutch colonial artifacts from the Hudson Valley area, and the 18th-century **Amstel House,** once the home of the seventh governor of Delaware, Nicholas Van Dyke (1738–1789), who was of Dutch descent.

Wilmington

Kalmar Nyckel
Wilmington
MAP 12 › B3

Old Swedes Church
606 North Church Street
in Wilmington
MAP 12 › B3

Farther upriver from New Castle is Wilmington, where Fort Christina was situated in what is now a park on the waterfront. It is also the home port of the *Kalmar Nyckel*, a replica of the Dutch-built ship that brought Pieter Minuit with his Swedes to the area in 1638. The **Old Swedes Church** survives as evidence of the Swedish settlement.

Beversrede Trail

A small road near Route 52
MAP 12 › B2

After Stuyvesant took over New Sweden in 1655, he petitioned the WIC directors to allow the Swedes to remain together rather than dispersing them and incurring their enmity. Swedish and Finnish settlements had actually spread northward to today's Philadelphia. Although the Swedes remained in effective control of the area along the Schuylkill, Stuyvesant attempted to show the Dutch flag by establishing a trading post called Beversrede along this fur-trading route. Today's **Beversrede Trail**, a small road close to Route 52, reminds us of this history of approximately 350 years ago.

Burlington Island

Finally, north of Philadelphia, Burlington Island (opposite Burlington, New Jersey) on the border with Pennsylvania must be noted as the location of the oldest Dutch trading post, Fort Wilhelmus, on the Delaware River. It was once considered a favorable site for the center of the Dutch colony. This idea was probably reconsidered the first time the Delaware froze, allowing Indians to cross the river on the ice. Fort Wilhelmus was abandoned in 1626 when New Netherland director Pieter Minuit decided to withdraw settlers from the outlying trading posts and concentrate them on the newly purchased island of Manhattan.

Johnson Ferry House

Passing Philadelphia, you may want to drive on to Trenton and from there northwest to Washington Crossing State Park, which marks the place where George Washington crossed the Delaware in 1776 to surprise the Hessian garrison in Trenton. The **Johnson Ferry House** at this site was originally built by Dutchman Rutger Jansen around 1740 and has several historic rooms.

355 Washington Crossing-Pennington Road (County Road 546) in Titusville
MAP 12 › D1

As you drive back north, U.S. 1, which leads from Trenton to Elizabeth, follows a well-worn overland Indian trail connecting Manhattan with the South River. It is reported that Indian runners could cover the ground in two days, rivaling today's mail-delivery schedule.

LIST OF SITES

Sites are generally listed in order of their appearance in the main texts (sites mentioned in the sidebars may be found in the index); listing does not include sites, streets, squares, parks, monuments, and statues that are outside/always accessible. Information on open days and hours is subject to change, so it is best to call ahead of time.

New York City

Manhattan/New Amsterdam:
Downtown Manhattan

Congregation Shearith Israel Synagogue
8 West 70th Street
New York, NY 10023
(212) 873-0300
Website: shearith-israel.org

Beth Haim Cemetery of Congregation
Shearith Israel
76 West 11th Street
New York, NY 10003
(212) 873-0300
E-mail: office@shearithisrael.org
Website: shearith-israel.org
Hours: By appointment only

West End Collegiate Church
368 West End Avenue
New York, NY 10024
(212) 787-1566
Website: westendchurch.org

Fraunces Tavern Museum
54 Pearl Street
New York, NY 10004
(212) 425-1778
Website: frauncestavernmuseum.org
Hours: Monday–Saturday, 12 p.m.–5 p.m.

**United States Custom House/Gustave
Heye Center, National Museum of the
American Indian**
1 Bowling Green
New York, NY 10004
(212) 514-3767
Hours: Sunday–Wednesday,
Friday–Saturday, 10 a.m.–5 p.m.;
Thursday, 10 a.m.–8 p.m.

North of New Amsterdam: Manhattan

St. Paul's Chapel of Trinity Church
209 Broadway, between Fulton
and Vesey Streets
New York, NY 10007
(212) 602-0874
Website: trinitywallstreet.org/
congregation/spc

St. Mark's Church-in-the-Bowery
131 East 10th Street
New York, NY 10003
(212) 674-6377
E-mail: office@stmarksbowery.org
Website: stmarksbowery.org
Hours: (East yard) 8:30 a.m.–9 p.m.;
(West yard) open in the warm weather
months; (Church office) Monday–Friday,
10 a.m.–4 p.m.

The New-York Historical Society
170 Central Park West, at 77th Street
New York, NY 10024
(212) 873-3400
E-mail: webmaster@nyhistory.org
Website: nyhistory.org
Hours: Tuesday–Saturday, 10 a.m.–6 p.m.;
Sunday, 11 a.m.–5:45 p.m.; Friday night,
open until 8 p.m.

The Metropolitan Museum of Art
1000 Fifth Avenue, at 82nd Street
New York, NY 10028
(212) 535-7710
TTY: (212) 570-3828
Website: metmuseum.org
Hours: Closed Monday (except holiday
Mondays); Tuesday–Thursday, 9:30
a.m.–5:30 p.m.; Friday and Saturday,
9:30 a.m.–9:00 p.m.; Sunday, 9:30 a.m.–
5:30 p.m.

Museum of the City of New York
1220 Fifth Avenue, between 103rdand
104th Streets
New York, NY 10029
(212) 534-1672
E-mail: info@mcny.org
Website: mcny.org
Hours: Closed Monday (except holiday
Mondays); Tuesday–Sunday, 10 a.m.–5 p.m.

Elmendorf Reformed Church
171 East 121st Street
New York, NY 10035
(212) 534-5856
E-mail: Elmendorf10035@msn.com
Website: churches.rca.org/elmendorf

459 West 144th Street, between
Convent and Amsterdam Avenues
New York, NY 10031
Privately owned

Dyckman Farmhouse Museum
4881 Broadway, at 204th Street
New York, NY 10034
(212) 304-9422
E-mail: info@dyckmanfarmhouse.org
Website: dyckmanfarmhouse.org
Hours: Wednesday–Saturday, 11 a.m.–
4 p.m.; Sunday, 12 p.m.–4 p.m.

North of New Amsterdam: Bronx

Van Cortlandt House Museum
Broadway at West 246th Street
Bronx, NY 10471
(718) 543-3344
Website: vancortlandthouse.org
Hours: Tuesday–Friday, 10 a.m.–3 p.m.;
Saturday–Sunday, 11 a.m.–4 p.m.
Call to confirm hours

Queens and Nassau Counties

**Vander Ende-Onderdonk House/
Greater Ridgewood Historical Society**
1820 Flushing Avenue,
near Onderdonk Avenue
Ridgewood, NY 11385
(718) 456-1776
Website: onderdonkhouse.org
Hours: Saturday, 1 p.m.–5 p.m.,
and by appointment

**Lent-Riker-Smith Homestead
and Cemetery**
78-03 19th Road, near LaGuardia airport
East Elmhurst, NY 11370
Privately owned

John Bowne House
The Bowne House Historical Society
37-01 Bowne Street
Flushing, NY 11354
(718) 359-0528
E-mail: office@bownehouse.org
Website: bownehouse.org
Hours: At this writing, the house is
closed for restoration. Group visits to
grounds and gardens may be arranged
with advance notice.

Friends Meetinghouse
137-16 Northern Boulevard
Flushing, NY 11354
(718) 261-9832
Website: nyym.org/flushing
Hours: Call for information

**Adriance Farmhouse/
Queens County Farm Museum**
73-50 Little Neck Parkway
Floral Park, NY 11004
(718) 347-3276
Website: queensfarm.org
Hours: Monday–Friday, 10 a.m.–5 p.m.
(exterior visits only); Saturday–Sunday,
10 a.m.–5 p.m.

Van Nostrand/Starkins House
20 Main Street
Roslyn, NY 11576
(516) 484-1643
Hours: Open May to October
For more information, contact the Roslyn
Landmark Society at (516) 625-4363 or
rlsinfo@optimum.net.

Roslyn Grist Mill
1347 Old Northern Boulevard
Roslyn, NY 11576
At this writing, the mill is awaiting
restoration and closed to the public.
For more information, contact the Roslyn
Landmark Society at (516) 625-4363 or
rlsinfo@optimum.net.

Old Bethpage Village Restoration
1303 Round Swamp Road (Exit 48 off the
Long Island Expressway)
Old Bethpage, NY 11804
(516) 572-8400
Hours: (April–December) Wednesday–
Sunday, 10 a.m.–4 p.m. (No one admitted
one hour before closing.) For more
information, call (516) 572-8401.

*The Minne Schenck House and Carlyle
Barn are located at Old Bethpage Village
Restoration.*

Hofstra University
900 Fulton Avenue
Hempstead, NY 11549
(516) 463-6600
Website: hofstra.edu

Brooklyn

Brooklyn Museum of Art
200 Eastern Parkway
Brooklyn, NY 11238
(718) 638-5000
TTY: (718) 399-8440
E-mail: information@brooklynmuseum.org
Website: brooklynmuseum.org
Hours: Wednesday, 11 a.m.-6 p.m.;
Thursday-Friday, 11 a.m.-10 p.m.;
Saturday-Sunday, 11 a.m.-6 p.m.;
first Saturday of each month,
11 a.m.-11 p.m.

*The Jan Martense Schenck and Nicholas
Schenck Houses are located in the period
rooms section of the Brooklyn Museum.*

Brooklyn Public Library (Central Library)
10 Grand Army Plaza, at Flatbush Avenue
and Eastern Parkway
Brooklyn, NY 11238
(718) 230-2100
Website: brooklynpubliclibrary.org
Hours: Monday-Thursday, 9 a.m.-9 p.m.;
Friday-Saturday, 10 a.m.-6 p.m.;
Saturday, 10 a.m.-6 p.m.; Sunday,
1 p.m.-5 p.m.

Lefferts Historic House
452 Flatbush Avenue, at Flatbush and
Ocean Avenues and Eastern Parkway
Brooklyn, NY 11225
(718) 789-2822
Website: prospectpark.org/visit/places/
lefferts
Hours: Vary with the seasons, call for
information

Reformed Church of Flatbush
890 Flatbush Avenue
Brooklyn, NY 11226
(718) 284-5140
Website: flatbushchurch.org

Erasmus Hall Academy/High School
911 Flatbush Avenue
Brooklyn, NY 11226
(718) 282-7804
Website: erasmushall.org
Not open to the general public

**Pieter Claesen Wyckoff House/
Wyckoff Farmhouse Museum**
5816 Clarendon Road
Brooklyn, NY 11203
(718) 629-5400
E-mail: info@wyckoffassociation.org
Website: wyckoffassociation.org
Hours: (May-October) grounds open
Tuesday-Sunday, 10 a.m.-4 p.m.;
(November 1-April 30) museum open
Tuesday-Saturday, 10 a.m.-4 p.m.

Joost Van Nuyse House
1128 East 34th Street
Brooklyn, NY 11210
Privately owned

Van Nuyse-Magaw House
1041 East 29th Street
Brooklyn, NY 11210
Privately owned

Flatlands Reformed Church
3931 Kings Highway
Brooklyn, NY 11234
(718) 252-5540
Website: flatlandsreformedchurch.org

Stoothoff-Baxter-Kouwenhoven House
1640 East 48th Street
Brooklyn, NY 11234
Privately owned

Hendrick I. Lott House
1940 East 36th Street
E-mail: hilhpa@lotthouse.org
Website: lotthouse.org
At this writing, the house is awaiting
restoration and closed to the public.

Salt Marsh Nature Center
2071 Flatbush Avenue
(entrance on Avenue U)
Brooklyn, NY 11229
(347) 701-8674
Website: saltmarshalliance.org
Hours: Daily except Wednesday,
11 a.m.-5 p.m.

Wyckoff-Bennett House
1662 East 22nd Street
Brooklyn, NY 11229
Privately owned

Elias Hubbard-Ryder House
1926 East 28th Street, between
Avenue S and Avenue T
Brooklyn, NY 11229
Privately owned

Gravesend Cemetery
Gravesend Neck Road, near Avenue V
at Van Sicklen Street
Hours: Tours may be booked through
the park rangers at the Salt Marsh
Nature Center.

Lady Moody (Van Sicklen) House
27 Gravesend Neck Road, at Avenue V near
Van Sicklen Street
Brooklyn, NY 11223
Privately owned

Ryder-Van Cleef House
38 Village Road North
Brooklyn, NY 11223
Privately owned

Hubbard House
2138 McDonald Avenue
Brooklyn, NY 11223
Privately owned

New Lots Reformed Churchyard
978 Schenck Avenue
Brooklyn, NY 11207
(718) 257-3455

New Utrecht Cemetery
16th Avenue and 84th Street at
18th Avenue
Brooklyn, NY 11214
Hours: Tours may be booked through
New Utrecht Reformed Church.

New Utrecht Reformed Church
1827 84th Street
Brooklyn, NY 11214
(718) 232-9500

Green-Wood Cemetery
1603 Greenwood Street
(407) 246-2616
Website: greenwood-cemetery.net
Hours: Daily, 7 a.m.-7 p.m.

Old Stone House (Historic Interpretive Center)
Washington Park/J.J. Byrne Playground
336 3rd Street
Brooklyn, NY 11215
(718) 768-3195
E-mail: info@theoldstonehouse.org
Website: theoldstonehouse.org
Hours: Saturday-Sunday, 11 a.m.-4 p.m.,
and by appointment

Brooklyn Historical Society
128 Pierrepont Street, at Clinton Street
Brooklyn, NY 11201
(718) 222-4111
Website: brooklynhistory.org
Hours: Wednesday-Friday, 12 p.m.-5 p.m.;
Saturday, 10 a.m.-5 p.m.;
Sunday, 12 p.m.-5 p.m.

Staten Island

Billiou-Stillwell-Perine House
1476 Richmond Road
Staten Island, NY 10304
Hours: For tours, contact Staten Island
Historical Society at (718) 351-1611.

Moravian Cemetery, New Dorp
2205 Richmond Road
Staten Island, NY 10306
(718) 351-0136
E-mail: moraviancemetery@gmail.com
Website: moraviancemetery.com
Hours: Monday-Sunday, 8 a.m.-6:30 p.m.,
conditions permitting

Historic Richmond Town
441 Clarke Avenue
Staten Island, NY 10306
(718) 351-1611
Website: historicrichmondtown.org
Hours: (July-August) Wednesday-
Sunday, 11 a.m.-5 p.m.; (September-
June) Wednesday-Sunday, 1 p.m.-5 p.m.

The Christopher House, Guyon-Lake-Tysen House and the Voorlezer's House are located in Historic Richmond Town.

Staten Island Reformed Church
54 Port Richmond Avenue
Staten Island, NY 10302
(718) 442-7393

Alice Austen House
2 Hylan Boulevard
Staten Island, NY 10305
(718) 816-4506
Website: aliceausten.org
Hours: House open March-December,
Thursday-Sunday, 12 p.m.-5 p.m.;
grounds open daily until dusk

Hudson Valley

East of the Hudson River, Traveling North

Philipse Manor Hall
29 Warburton Avenue
Yonkers, NY 10701
(914) 965-4027
E-mail: PhilipseManorHall@gmail.com
Website: philipsemanorhall.blogspot.com
Hours: (Open for guided tours only)
Wednesday–Friday, 1 p.m., 2 p.m., and 3
p.m.; Saturday–Sunday, 11 a.m., 12 p.m.,
1 p.m., 2 p.m., and 3 p.m.; closed on all
federal and state holidays

Sunnyside
9 West Sunnyside Lane
Irvington, NY 10533
(914) 591-5493
Website: hudsonvalley.org/content/
view/13/43
Hours: (April 1–Oct. 31) daily except
Tuesday, 10 a.m.–5 p.m.
For more information, call (914) 631-8200
(Monday–Friday) or (914) 591-8763
(weekends).

Philipsburg Manor
381 North Broadway
Sleepy Hollow, NY 10591
(914) 631-3992
Website: hudsonvalley.org/content/
view/14/44
Hours: (April 1–Oct. 31) daily except
Tuesday, 10 a.m.–5 p.m.
For more information, call (914) 631-8200
(Monday–Friday) or (914) 631-3992
(weekends).

The Sleepy Hollow Church
540 North Broadway
Sleepy Hollow, NY 10591
(914) 631-0081
E-mail: info@sleepyhollowcemetary.org
Website: sleepyhollowcemetery.org
Cemetery Hours: Monday–Friday,
8 a.m.–4:30 p.m.; Saturday–Sunday,
8:30 a.m.–4:30 p.m.

Kykuit
Tickets: Philipsburg Manor
381 North Broadway (Route 9)
Sleepy Hollow, NY 10591
(914) 631-3992
Website: hudsonvalley.org/content/
view/12/42
Hours: (Early May–early November) daily
except Tuesday;Tickets may be obtained
at Philipsburg Manor, 381 North Broadway.
For more information, call (914) 631-8200
(Monday–Friday) or (914) 631-3992
(weekends).

Van Cortlandt Manor
500 South Riverside Avenue
Croton-on-Hudson, NY 10520
(914) 271-8981
Website: hudsonvalley.org/content/
view/15/45
Hours: (Late May–Labor Day weekend)
Thursday–Sunday and Monday holidays,
10 a.m.–5 p.m.; (October and November)
for schedule, call (914) 631-8200
(Monday–Friday) or (914) 271-8981
(weekends)

**Hudson Valley Center
for Contemporary Art**
1701 Main Street
Peekskill, NY 10566
(914) 788-0100
E-mail: info@hvcca.org
Website: hvcca.org
Hours: Saturday–Sunday, 12 p.m.–
6 p.m., and by appointment

Boscobel
1601 Route 9D
Garrison, NY 10524
(845) 265-3638
E-mail: info@boscobel.org
Website: boscobel.org
Hours: (April–October) daily except
Tuesday, 9:30 a.m.–5 p.m.;
(November–December) 9:30 a.m.–4 p.m.

Madam Brett Homestead Museum
50 Van Nydeck Avenue
Beacon, NY 12508
(845) 831-6533
Hours: (April–December) by
appointment only, second Saturday
of the month, 1 p.m.–4 p.m.

Mount Gulian Historic Site
145 Sterling Street
Beacon, NY 12508
(845) 831–8172
Website: mountgulian.org
Hours: (Mid-April–end of October)
Wednesday, Thursday, Friday, and
Sunday, 1 p.m.–5 p.m.

Van Wyck Homestead Museum
504 Route 9
Fishkill, NY 12524
(845) 896–9560
E-mail: webmaster@fishkillridge.org
Website: fishkillridge.org/history/vanwyck.
htm
Hours: (June–October) Saturday–Sunday,
1 p.m.–4 p.m.; museum and library also
open by appointment

Brinckerhoff-Pudney-Palen House
68 Kensington Drive
Hopewell Junction, NY 12533
(845) 227–4136
Website: eastfishkillhistoricalsociety.org
Hours: Open houses and special events
throughout the year

Hendrick Kip House
NYS Route 308, Southwest of Route 52
Glenham-Fishkill
Privately owned

Colonel John Brinckerhoff House
Lomala Road, off Route 82
Fishkill, NY 12524
Privately owned

Storm-Adriance-Brinckerhoff House
Beekman Road (Route 9)
East Fishkill, NY 12533
Privately owned

The Frances Lehman Loeb Art Center
124 Raymond Avenue, Box 703
Poughkeepsie, NY 12604
(845) 437–7745
Website: fllac.vassar.edu
Hours: Monday–Wednesday,
10 a.m.–5 p.m.; Thursday, 10 a.m.–
9 p.m.; Friday–Saturday, 10 a.m.–
5 p.m.; Sunday, 1 p.m.–5 p.m.

Hyde Park/Springwood
4097 Albany Post Road
Hyde Park, NY 12538
(845) 229–9115
Website: nps.gov/hofr
Hours: Grounds open daily, year-round,
sunrise to sunset; house open daily for
guided tours only, 9 a.m.–5 p.m.

Val-Kill
56 Valkill Park Road
Hyde Park, NY 12538
(845) 229–5302
Website: nps.gov/elro
Hours: Grounds open daily, year-round,
sunrise to sunset. (May–October) house
open for guided tours 9 a.m.–5 p.m. (last
tour at 4 p.m.); (November–April) tours
offered Thursday-Monday, 1 p.m. and 3
p.m.; closed Tuesday–Wednesday.
For more information, call 845–229–9422.

Top Cottage
15 Valkill Drive
Hyde Park, NY 12538
Hours: (May–October) daily; tours begin
at the Henry A. Wallace Visitor Center.
For reservations and more information,
call (845) 229–5320.

Frederick W. and Louise
Vanderbilt Mansion
81 Vanderbilt Park Road
Hyde Park, NY 12538
*For computer driving instructions, use 4097
Albany Post Road, Hyde Park, NY 12538*
(845) 229–7770
For tour information, call (845) 486–1966
(Monday–Friday).

The Beekman Arms
Route 9/6387 Mill Street
Rhinebeck, NY 12572
(845) 876–7077
Website: beekmandelamaterinn.com/
restaurant.htm

Montgomery Place
8 Davis Way
Annandale-on-Hudson, NY
Privately owned

Clermont State Historic Site
One Clermont Avenue
Germantown, NY 12526
(518) 537–4240
E-mail: fofc@gtel.net
Website: friendsofclermont.org
Hours: Open seasonally, call for information

Jan Van Hoesen House
Dutch Village Mobile Home Park
440 Route 66
Hudson, New York 12534
Privately owned

Van Dusen House
County Road 29/Spook Rock Road
Claverack, New York 12443
Privately owned

Lindenwald
Route 9H/Old Post Road,
near Albany Avenue
Kinderhook, NY 12106
Website: nps.gov/mava
Hours: (Mid-May–end of October) daily,
9 a.m.–5 p.m.

Luykas Van Alen House
Route 9H, about one mile south of
Kinderhook center
Kinderhook, NY 12106
(518) 758-9265
Website: cchsny.org
Hours: (End of May through early October)
open weekends

Crailo State Historic Site
9 1/2 Riverside Avenue, between Aiken
Avenue and Belmore Place
Rensselaer, NY 12144
(518) 463-8738
Hours: (Mid-April–October 31)
Wednesday–Sunday, 11 a.m.–4 p.m.;
(June, July, and August) also open on
Tuesdays; (November–mid-April) open by
appointment only

**Knickerbocker Historical Society/
Knickerbocker Mansion**
132 Knickerbocker Road
Schaghticoke, NY 12154
(518) 664-1700
Website: knic.com/historic.htm
Hours: Call for information

Albany

First Church of Albany
110 North Pearl Street
Albany, NY 12201
(518) 463-4449
Hours: Call for information

Quackenbush House
25 Quackenbush Square
Albany, NY 12207
Privately owned, operated as a restaurant

The Albany Institute of History and Art
125 Washington Avenue
Albany, NY 12210
(518) 463-4478
E-mail: information@albanyinstitute.org
Website: albanyinstitute.org
Hours: Wednesday–Saturday, 10 a.m.–
5 p.m.; Sunday, 12 p.m.–5 p.m.

New York State Museum
Cultural Education Center
222 Madison Avenue
Albany, NY 12230
(518) 474-5877
Website: nysm.nysed.gov
Hours: Monday–Saturday,
9:30 a.m.–5 p.m.

**New Netherland Institute/
New York State Library**
Cultural Education Center,
Room 10D45
222 Madison Avenue
Albany, NY 12230
(518) 486-4815
Website: nnp.org
Hours: By appointment only

**Ten Broeck Mansion/Albany
Historical Association**
9 Ten Broeck Place
Albany, NY 12210
(518) 436-9826
Website: sites.google.com/site/
tenbroeckmansion
Hours: (May–December) open for tours
Thursday and Friday, 10 a.m.–4 p.m.;
Saturday and Sunday, 1 p.m.–4 p.m.

Schuyler Mansion State Historic Site
32 Catherine Street
Albany, NY 12202
(518) 434-0834
Website: nysparks.state.ny.us/historic-
sites/33
Hours: (May 15–October 31) Wednesday-
Sunday, 11 a.m.–5 p.m. (last tour begins at 4
p.m.); (November through mid-May) tours
available by appointment only

Historic Cherry Hill
523 1/2 South Pearl Street
Albany, NY 12202
(518) 434-4791
E-mail: info@historiccherryhill.org
Website: historiccherryhill.org
Hours: (April to December) Wednesday
and Saturday afternoons, behind-the-
scenes restoration tours are offered to the
public by appointment

Schenectady

Schenectady County Historical Society
32 Washington Avenue
Schenectady, NY 12305
(518) 374-0263
Website: schist.org
Hours: Monday–Friday, 9 a.m.–5 p.m.;
Thursday, 5–8 p.m.; Saturday,
10 a.m.–2 p.m.

Isaac Vrooman House
31 Front Street
Schenectady, NY 12305
Privately owned

29 Front Street
Schenectady, NY 12305
Privately owned

Johannes Teller House
121 Front Street
Schenectady, NY 12305
Privately owned

109 Union Street
Schenectady, NY 12305
Privately owned

Hendrick Brouwer House
14 North Church Street
Schenectady, NY 12305
Privately owned

Mabee Farm Historic Site
1080 Main Street (Route 5S)
Rotterdam Junction, NY 12150
(518) 887-5073
E-mail: mabeefarm@gmail.com
Website: schist.org/mabee.htm
Hours: (May-September) Tuesday-
Saturday, 10 a.m.-4 p.m., and by
appointment year-round

Arent Bradt Residence
22 Schermerhorn Road
Schenectady, NY 12306
Privately owned

Schermerhorn Homestead
47 Schermerhorn Road
Schenectady, NY 12306
Privately owned

Dellemont-Wemple Farm
268 Wemple Road
Schenectady, NY 12306
Privately owned

West of the Hudson River, Traveling South

Ariaantje Coeymans Stone House
28 Stonehouse Hill Road
Coeymans, NY
Privately owned

Tobias Ten Eyk House and Cemeteries
Old Ravena Road, north of
the Route 9W junction
Coeymans, NY
Privately owned

Bronck Museum
Route 9W, on Pieter Bronck Road
Coxsackie, NY 12051
(518) 731-6490
Website: gchsbm@mhcable.com
Hours: (Memorial Day weekend to
mid-October) scheduled guided tours
Wednesday-Friday, 12-4 p.m.; Saturday
and Monday holidays, 10 a.m.-4 p.m.;
Sunday, 1 p.m.-4 p.m.

Kiersted House Museum
119 Main Street
Saugerties, NY 12477
(845) 246-9529
Website: saugertieshistoricalsociety.com/
main.html
Hours: (Memorial Day-October) Saturday
and Sunday, 1 p.m.-4 p.m., and by
appointment

Old Dutch Church Heritage Museum
272 Wall Street
Kingston, NY 12401
(845) 338-6759
Website: olddutchchurch.org/museum.php
Hours: Sunday, 10:30 a.m. and 12:30 p.m.,
and by appointment; self-guided, walking-
tour brochures are available at the church
and by mail

Hoffman House Restaurant
94 North Front Street
Kingston, NY 12401
(845) 338-2626

Senate House
296 Fair Street, at North Front Street
and Clinton Avenue
Stockade District
Kingston, NY 12401
(845) 338-2786
Hours: Building and grounds are open to
the public; Senate House staff provides
guided tours

Klyne Esopus Historical Society Museum
764 Broadway/Route 9W
Ulster Park, NY 12487
(845) 338-8109
Website: klyneesopusmuseum.org
Hours: (Early June-late November)
Friday-Monday, 1 p.m.-4 p.m.

Hurley Heritage Society Museum
52 Main Street
Hurley, New York 12443
(845) 338-1661
E-mail: HHS1661@hurleyheritagesociety.
org
Website: hurleyheritagesociety.org
Hours: (May–October) Saturday, 10 a.m.–
4 p.m.; Sunday, 1 p.m.–4 p.m.

**Bevier House Museum/Ulster
County Historical Society**
Physical address:
2682 Route 209
Marbletown, NY
Mailing address:
Ulster County Historical Society
Post Office Box 279
Stone Ridge, New York 12484
(845) 338-5614
Website: bevierhousemuseum.org
Hours: (May 1–end of October)
Thursday–Sunday, 12 p.m.–5 p.m.

Historic Huguenot Street
81 Huguenot Street, between North Front
Street and Broadhead Avenue
New Paltz, NY 12561
(845) 255-1889
E-mail: info@huguenotstreet.org
Website: huguenotstreet.org
Hours: (April) Saturday and Sunday,
11 a.m.–3 p.m.; (May–October)
Monday–Tuesday, Thursday–Sunday, 10:30
a.m.–5 p.m.; (November and December)
Saturday and Sunday, 11 a.m.–3 p.m.

*The Dubois Fort/Historic Huguenot Street
Visitor Center, Jean Hasbrouck House,
Bevier-Elting House, Ezekiel Elting House,
Deyo House, Abraham Hasbrouck House,
Freer House, French Church, and Old
Huguenot Burial Ground are all located on
Historic Huguenot Street.*

Hasbrouck House
84 Liberty Street
New Paltz, NY 12561
Privately owned

Dutch Reformed Church
134 Grand Street
Newburgh, NY 12550

**Jacob Blauvelt House/Historical Society
of Rockland County**
20 Zukor Road
New City, NY 10956
(845) 634-9629
Website: rocklandhistory.org
Gallery hours during exhibitions:
Wednesday–Sunday, 12 p.m.–4 p.m.

DeWint House/George Washington
Headquarters
Livingston Street and Oak Tree Road
Tappan, NY 10983
(845) 359-1359
Website: dewinthouse.com
Hours: Tuesday–Sunday, 10 a.m.–
4 p.m.; Call in advance of visit

New Jersey and Delaware

Northern New Jersey:
Bergen and Passaic Counties

Von Steuben House (Zabriskie-Von Steuben House)/Bergen County Historical Society
1209 Main Street
River Edge, NJ 07661
(201) 343-9492
Website: bergencountyhistory.org
Hours: Open for special events

Campbell-Christie House
1201 Main Street
River Edge, NJ 07661
Hours: Open for special events sponsored by the Bergen County Historical Society

Demarest House
Main Street
River Edge, NJ 07661
For more information, contact the Blauvelt Demarest Foundation at (201) 261-0012 or 705 Kinderkamack Road, Oradell, NJ 07649.

Derick Banta House
180 Washington Avenue
Dumont, NJ 07628
Privately owned

Roelof Westervelt House
256 Tenafly Road, near
Westervelt Avenue
Tenafly, NJ 07670
Privately owned
Haring-De Wolf House
95 De Wolf Road
Old Tappan, NJ 07675
Privately owned

Garretson Forge and Farm
4-02 River Road
Fair Lawn, NJ 07410
(551) 206-4380
Website: garretsonfarm.org
Hours: (April–December) Sunday,
1 p.m.–4 p.m., and by appointment

Garretson Farm is owned by Bergen County and is administered by volunteers of the Garretson Forge and Farm Restoration, Inc.

Wortendyke Barn Museum
13 Pascack Road
Park Ridge, NJ 07656
(201) 336-7267
Hours: (April–October) Wednesday,
Saturday, and Sunday, 12 p.m.–4 p.m.

Saddle River Reformed Church/ Old Stone Church Historic Site
500 East Saddle River Road
Upper Saddle River, NJ 07458
(201) 327-5242

Hopper-Goetschius House
245 Lake Street
Upper Saddle River, NJ
(201) 327-8644
Hours: (July and August) Sunday,
2 p.m.–4 p.m., and by appointment
The Van Riper-Tice Barn is also located on this site.

Laroe-Van Horn House
398 Ramapo Valley Road
Mahwah, NJ 07430
Privately owned

Hendrick Van Allen House
13–15 Ramapo Valley Road
Oakland, NJ 07436
(201) 405-7726
Hours: Usually open the third Sunday of each month, 1 p.m.–4 p.m.

Jacobus S. Demarest House
3 Dogwood Drive
Oakland, NJ 07436
Privately owned

Van Voorhees-Quackenbush-Zabriskie House/Municipal Museum
421 Franklin Avenue
Wyckoff, NJ 07481
(201) 891-0057
Hours: (School year) Friday,
9 a.m.–3:00 p.m.; also open for special events and holiday tours

Wyckoff Reformed Church
580 Wyckoff Avenue
Wyckoff, NJ 07481
(201) 891-1782

Dey Mansion
199 Totowa Road
Wayne, NJ 07470
(973) 696-1776
Hours: (Office) Wednesday–Friday,
9 a.m.–4 p.m.; Saturday and Sunday,
10 a.m.–4 p.m. (Tours) Wednesday–Friday,
1 p.m.–4 p.m.; Saturday and Sunday, 10
a.m.–12 p.m. and 1 p.m.–4 p.m. (last tour
3:30 p.m.)

Schuyler Colfax House Museum
2343 Hamburg Turnpike
Wayne, NJ 07470
(973) 694-7192
The house is currently undergoing
restoration and is closed to the public.

Van Riper-Hopper House
533 Berdan Avenue
Wayne, NJ 07470
(973) 694-7192
Hours: The house is part of a museum
complex that also includes the Mead-Van
Duyne House: both houses are open by
appointment only.

Mead-Van Duyne House
533 Berdan Avenue
Wayne, NJ 07470
(973) 694-7192
Hours: The house is part of a museum
complex that also includes the Van Riper-
Hopper House; both houses are open by
appointment only.

Hamilton-Van Wagoner House
971 Valley Road
Clifton, NJ 07013
(973) 744-5707
Hours: (March–December) Sunday,
2 p.m.–4 p.m., except holiday weekends;
also open by appointment

The Delaware Water Gap:
Sussex and Warren Counties

Abraham Van Campen Farmhouse
Millbrook Village
E-mail: mailto@millbrooknj.com
Website: millbrooknj.com
Hours: Village open daily, year-round;
various buildings are open on weekends,
as scheduled
For more information, call the National
Park Service at (570) 426-2435.

Van Campen Barn
Millbrook Village
E-mail: mailto@millbrooknj.com
Website: millbrooknj.com
Hours: Village open daily, year-round;
various buildings are open on weekends,
as scheduled
For more information, call the National
Park Service at (570) 426-2435.

**Issac Van Campen House /Van
Campen Inn**
Old Mine Road (National Park Service
Road 605), north of Millbrook Village
Walpack Township, NJ
Hours: Seasonal
For more information, call the Walpack
Historical Society at (973) 948-6671.

Westbrook-Bell House
Old Mine Road (County Road 521)
Sandyston Township, NJ
Privately owned

**(Reverend Elias) Van Bunschooten House/
DAR Van Bunschooten Museum**
1097 Route 23
Wantage, New Jersey 07461
(973) 875-4058 or (973) 875-5335
Hours: (May 15–October 15) Thursday
and Saturday, 1 p.m.–4 p.m., and by
appointment

Central New Jersey: Hudson, Monmouth,
Middlesex, and Somerset Counties

**Apple Tree House/
Van Wagenen Homestead**
298 Academy Street
Jersey City, NJ
Website: appletreehouse.org
At this writing, the house has been
closed for several years.

Sip Manor House
5 Cherry Lane
Westfield, NJ 07090
Privately owned

Old Bergen Church
1 Highland Avenue
Jersey City, NJ 07306
(201) 433-1815
Website: oldbergenchurch.org

Summit House/Newkirk House
510 Summit Avenue
Jersey City, NJ 07087
Privately owned

Van Vorst House
531 Palisade Avenue
Jersey City, NJ 07307
Privately owned

Holmes-Hendrickson House
62 Longstreet Road
Holmdel, NJ 07733
Hours: (May–September)
Thursday–Saturday, 1 p.m.–4 p.m.
For more information, call the
Monmouth County Historical Society
at (732) 462-1466.

Longstreet Farm
50 Longstreet Road
Holmdel, NJ 07333
(732) 946-3758
Hours: (March–December) farm open
weekends and holidays,12 p.m.–3:30 p.m.,
and by reservation; (Memorial Day to Labor
Day) grounds open daily, 9 a.m.–5 p.m.;
(Labor Day to Memorial Day) grounds open
daily, 10 a.m.–4 p.m.

Covenhoven House
150 West Main Street
Freehold, NJ 07728
Hours: (May–September) Thursday–
Saturday, 1 p.m.–4 p.m.
For more information, call the
Monmouth County Historical Society
at (732) 462-1466.

First Reformed Church
9 Bayard Street
New Brunswick, NJ 08901
(732) 545-1005
Hours: Call for information

Rutgers University
536 George Street
New Brunswick, NJ 08901
(732) 445-4636

(Gardner A.) Sage Library,
New Brunswick Theological Seminary
21 Seminary Place
New Brunswick, NJ 08901
(732) 247-5241

Metlar-Bodine House Museum
1281 River Road
Piscataway, NJ 08854
(732) 463-8363
At this writing, the house is
undergoing restoration.

Cornelius Low House/
Middlesex County Museum
1225 River Road
Piscataway, NJ 08854
(732) 745-4177
Hours: Tuesday–Friday, 1 p.m.–4 p.m.;
Sunday 1 p.m.–4 p.m.

East Jersey Olde Towne Village
1050 River Road
Piscataway, NJ 08854
(732) 745-3030
Hours: Tuesday–Friday, 8:30 a.m.–
4:15 p.m.; Sunday, 1 p.m.–4 p.m.

A re-creation of the Church at Three-Mile
Run and the restored Jacobus Vanderveer
House are located in this village.

Van Wickle House
1289 Easton Avenue
Somerset, NJ 07783
Hours: For more information, call the
Meadows Foundation at (732) 828-7418.

Wyckoff Garretson House
215 South Middlebush Road
Somerset, NJ 08873
Hours: For more information, call the
Meadows Foundation at (732) 828-7418.

Van Liew-Suydam House
280 South Middlebush Road
Somerset, NJ 08873
Hours: For more information, call the
Meadows Foundation at (732) 828-7418.

Hageman House and Farm
209 South Middlebush Road
Somerset, NJ 08873
Hours: For more information, call the
Meadows Foundation at (732) 828-7418.

Franklin Inn/Annie Van Liew House
2371 Amwell Road
Somerset, NJ 08873
(732) 828-7418
At this writing, the house is closed for
repairs.

Old Dutch Parsonage
38 Washington Place
Somerville, NJ 08876
Hours: Wednesday–Saturday, 10 a.m.–
12 p.m. and 1 p.m.–4 p.m.; Sunday, 1 p.m.–
4 p.m.; For more information, call the New
Jersey Department of Parks and Forests at
(908) 725-1015.

Wallace House
65 Washington Place
Somerville, NJ 08876
Hours: Wednesday–Saturday, 10 a.m.–
12 p.m. and 1 p.m.–4 p.m.; Sunday,
1 p.m–4 p.m.
For more information, call the
New Jersey Department of Parks
and Forests at (908) 725-1015.

Van Horne House
941 Main Street
Bridgewater, NJ 08807
(732) 356-8856
E-mail: info@heritagetrail.org
Website: heritagetrail.org
Hours: Open for special events and by
appointment

Van Veghten House
9 Van Veghten Drive
Bridgewater, NJ 08807
(908) 218-1281
Website: schsnj.com
Hours: (April 1–December 1) house and
library open the second Saturday of
each month, 12 p.m.–4 p.m.

Abraham Van Campen Homestead
East side of Old Mine Road, south of
Millbrook Village, about nine miles
north of the Delaware Water Gap
For more information, call the New
Jersey Department of Parks and
Forests at (908) 725-1015.

Delaware: Cape May to Burlington

Zwaanendael Museum
102 King's Highway at Savannah Road
Lewes, DE 19958
(302) 645-1148
Hours (subject to change):
Wednesday–Saturday, 10 a.m.–
4:30 p.m.; open on Labor Day,
Memorial Day, and July 4th

Ryves-Holt House/
Lewes Historical Society
110 Shipcarpenter Street
Lewes, DE 19958
(302) 645-7670
E-mail: info@historiclewes.org
Hours: Call or e-mail for information.

Bombay Hook National
Wildlife Refuge
2591 Whitehall Neck Road
Smyrna, DE 19977
(302) 653-6872
Website: fws.gov/northeast/bombayhook
Hours: Refuge open daily, year-round,
from sunrise to sunset. Part of the refuge is
closed for hunting 15 days of the year. Call
for visitor center hours.

Chesapeake and Delaware
Canal Museum
815 Bethel Road
Chesapeake City, MD 21915
(410) 885-5622
Hours: Monday–Friday, 8 a.m.–
4 p.m.; Saturday, 11 a.m.–3 p.m;
closed government holidays

Dutch House
32 East Third Street
New Castle, DE 19720
(302) 322-2794
Website: newcastlehistory.org/houses/
dutch.html
Hours: Wednesday–Saturday, 10 a.m.–
4 p.m.; Sunday, 12 p.m.–4 p.m.

Amstel House
2 East Fourth Street,
New Castle, DE 19720
(302) 322-2794
Website: newcastlehistory.org/houses/
visit.html
Hours: Wednesday–Saturday, 10 a.m.–
4 p.m.; Sunday, 12 p.m.–4 p.m.

Old Swedes Church
606 North Church Street
Wilmington, DE 19801
(302) 652-5629
E-mail: info@oldswedes.org
Website: oldswedes.org
Hours: (January–February) by appointment
only; (March) Wednesday–Friday, 1 p.m.–
4 p.m.; Saturday, 10 a.m.–4 p.m.;
(April–December) Wednesday–Saturday,
10 a.m.–4 p.m.

Johnson Ferry House
Washington Crossing State Park
355 Washington Crossing-Pennington
Road (County Road 546)
Titusville, NJ 08508
(609) 737-0609
Website: state.nj.us/dep/parksandforests/
parks/washcros.html
Hours: Wednesday–Saturday, 9 a.m.–
4 p.m.; Sunday, 1 p.m.–4 p.m.

ILLUSTRATION CREDITS

Title Page Map of New Netherland, with a view of New Amsterdam (now New-York) A.D. 1656 by Adriaen van der Donck, lithograph copied for *D.T. Valentine's Manual*, 1852 by Geo. Haywards. The New-York Historical Society

Page 12 Dietrich Gehring

Pages 14-15 The New-York Historical Society, bequest of Cora Van Rensselaer Catlin, 1915.7

Page 17 Mark Brown

Page 20 The Nationaal Archief, The Hague, The Netherlands

Page 23 The New York Public Library Picture Collection, The New York Public Library/Art Resource, NY

Page 27 Museum of the City of New York, gift of the Biblioteca Medicea-Laurenziana, Florence, Italy, 49.150

Page 28 The New-York Historical Society, bequest of Gerard Stuyvesant, 1922.99

Page 29 Bart Michiels

Page 31 Congregation Shearith Israel in the City of New York

Page 33 Het Nationaal Archief, The Hague, The Netherlands

Pages 34-35 The Citco Collection

Pages 36, 38, 39, 43, 45 Richard Koek

Page 46 Museum of the City of New York, gift of Miss Margaret S. Remsen, 69.64

Page 48 The Metropolitan Museum of Art, Marquand Collection, Gift of Henry G. Marquand, 1889 (89.15.21)

Page 49 The Metropolitan Museum of Art. Purchase, special contributions and funds given or bequeathed by friends of the Museum, 1961, 61.198

Page 51 (above) S. de Vries, 2008

Page 51 (below) Richard Koek

Page 53 Ocean/Corbis

Page 55 Spectrum Colour Library/ Heritage-Images/The Image Works

Page 58 S. de Vries, 2008

Page 59 Courtesy of Department of Parks, New York City

Page 61 FoodCollection/SuperStock

Page 65 Historic American Buildings Survey, Library of Congress

Page 67 (above) Ellen Brody-Kirmss

Page 67 (below) Marion Duckworth Smith

Page 69 Louie Psihoyos/Science Faction/ Corbis

Page 71 (both) Queens County Farm Museum

Page 73 (below) Department of Special Collections, Hofstra University

Page 79 Old Stone House Historic Interpretive Center

Page 80 The Brooklyn Museum of Art

Page 81 Prospect Park Alliance

Page 82 Brooklyn Collection, Brooklyn Public Library

Page 83 Richard Koek

Page 84 Wyckoff Farmhouse Museum

Page 91 (below) Richard Koek

Page 93 (above) Richard Koek

Page 93 (below) Brooklyn Historical Society

Page 94 Dietrich Gehring

Page 97 Richard Koek

Page 113 David Forbert/SuperStock

Page 120 Heleen Westerhuijs

Page 121 Danique Lodewijks

Pages 122-123 Bart Michiels

Page 124 Heleen Westerhuijs

Page 126 Mount Gulian Historic Site

Page 128 Lebrecht/The Image Works

Page 131 Richard Cheek

Page 132 WD Urbin, courtesy of the National Park Service

Page 136 Underwood & Underwood/Corbis

Page 137 Hulton Archive/Getty Images

Page 138 David Boyer/National Geographic Stock

Page 139 SuperStock/Getty

Page 141 Dietrich Gehring

Page 143 Manuscripts and Special Collections, New York State Library

Page 144 Albany Public Library

Page 144 Don Rittner

Pages 147, 151 Dietrich Gehring

Page 153 (below) Don Rittner

Pages 154, 155 Dietrich Gehring

Page 165 AAG Associates

Page 166 (above) France Menk

Page 166 (below) Geoffrey Gross

Page 168 Getty Images

Page 187 Robert Sisson/National Geographic Stock

Page 191 (below) The New-York Historical Society, gift of Dr. Fenwick Beekman, 1941.914

Page 192 The New-York Historical Society, gift of Robert Van Rensselaer Stuyvesant, 1909.34

Page 193 Museum of the City of New York, gift of Mrs. Augustus Van Cortlandt, 73.25

Page 197 (above) Leon Yost

Pages 203, 204 Nick Romanenko courtesy of Rutgers, The State University of New Jersey

Page 206 Smithsonian American Art Museum, Washington, DC/ Art Resource, NY

Page 207 HIP/Art Resource, NY

Page 212 Mark Else

BIBLIOGRAPHY

Archdeacon, Thomas J. *New York City, 1664–1710: Conquest and Change.* Ithaca: Cornell University Press, 1976.

Blackburn, Roderic H., and Geoffrey Gross. *Dutch Colonial Homes in America.* New York: Rizzoli International, 2002.

Blackburn, Roderic H., and Ruth Piwonka, eds. *Remembrance of Patria: Dutch Arts and Culture in Colonial America, 1609–1776.* Albany: Albany Institute of History and Art, 1988.

Burrows, Edwin G., and Mike Wallace. *Gotham: A History of New York City to 1898.* New York: Oxford University Press, 1999.

Cohen, David S. *The Dutch-American Farm.* New York and London: New York University Press, 1992.

Fabend, Firth Haring. *Zion on the Hudson: Dutch New York and New Jersey in the Age of Revivals.* New Brunswick: Rutgers University Press, 2000.

Fitchen, John. *The New World Dutch Barn.* Syracuse: Syracuse University Press, 1968.

Frijhoff, Willem. *Fulfilling God's Mission: The Two Worlds of Dominie Everardus Bogardus, 1606–1647.* Leiden and Boston: Brill, 2007.

Gehring, Charles T. *A Guide to Dutch Manuscripts Relating to New Netherland.* Albany: University of the State of New York, 1978.

Goodfriend, Joyce D. *Before the Melting Pot: Society and Culture in New York City, 1664–1730.* Princeton: Princeton University Press, 1992.

———, ed. *Revisiting New Netherland: Perspectives on Early Dutch America.* Leiden and Boston: Brill, 2005.

———, Benjamin Smith, and Annette Stott, eds. *Going Dutch: The Dutch Presence in America, 1609–2009.* Leiden and Boston: Brill, 2008.

Gosselink, Martine. *New York/New Amsterdam: The Dutch Origins of Manhattan.* Amsterdam: Nieuw Amsterdam Uitgevers/Nationaal Archief, 2009.

Grumet, Robert Steven. *Native American Place Names in New York City.* New York: Museum of the City of New York, 1981.

———. *Historic Contact: Indian People and Colonists in Today's Northeastern United States in the Sixteenth Through Eighteenth Centuries.* Norman, OK: University of Oklahoma Press, 1995.

Israel, Jonathan I. *The Dutch Republic.* New York: Oxford University Press, 1995.

Jacobs, Jaap. *The Colony of New Netherland: A Dutch Settlement in Seventeenth-Century America.* Ithaca: Cornell University Press, 2009.

Klooster, Wim. *The Dutch in the Americas, 1600–1800.* Providence: John Carter Brown Library, 1997.

Krabbendam, Hans, Cornelis A. Van Minnen, and Giles Scott-Smith, eds. *Four Centuries of Dutch-American Relations, 1609–2009.* Albany: SUNY Press, 2009.

Krewson, Margrit B. *New Netherland 1609–1664: A Selective Bibliography.* Washington D.C.: Library of Congress, 1995.

Krohn, Deborah L., and Peter N. Miller, with Marybeth De Fillipis, eds. *Dutch New York between East and West: The World of Margrieta van Varick.* New Haven and London: Yale University Press, 2009.

Meeske, Harrison. *The Hudson Valley Dutch and Their Houses.* Fleischmanns, NY: Purple Mountain Press, 2001. First published 1998.

Panetta, Roger, ed. *Dutch New York: The Roots of Hudson Valley Culture.* New York: Fordham University Press/Hudson River Museum, 2009.

Pritchard, Evan T. *Native New Yorkers: The Legacy of the Algonquin People of New York.* San Francisco/Tulsa: Council Oak Books, 2007.

Rose, Peter G. *Food, Drink and Celebrations of the Hudson Valley Dutch.* Charleston, SC: The History Press, 2009.

Shattuck, Martha Dickinson, ed. *Explorers, Fortunes, and Love Letters: A Window on New Netherland.* Albany: Mount Ida Press, 2009.

Shorto, Russell. *The Island at the Center of the World: The Epic Story of Dutch Manhattan and the Forgotten Colony that Shaped America.* New York: Doubleday, 2004.

Snow, Dean R., Charles T. Gehring, and William A. Starna, eds. *In Mohawk Country: Early Narratives about a Native People.* Syracuse: Syracuse University Press, 1996.

Stevens, John R. *Dutch Vernacular Architecture in North America, 1640–1830.* New York: The Society for the Preservation of Hudson Valley Vernacular Architecture, 2005.

Stott, Annette. *Holland Mania: The Unknown Dutch Period in American Art and Culture.* Woodstock: Overlook Press, 1998.

Van der Sijs, Nicoline. *Cookies, Coleslaw and Stoops: The Influence of Dutch on the North American Languages.* Amsterdam: Amsterdam University Press, 2009.

Venema, Janny. *Beverwijck: A Dutch Village on the American Frontier, 1652–1664.* Albany: SUNY Press, 2003.

———, *Kiliaen van Rensselaer (1586–1643): Designing a New World.* Albany: SUNY Press, 2011.

EDITORS' ACKNOWLEDGEMENTS

First of all, we would like to express our immense gratitude to Charles Gehring, Jaap Jacobs, and Robert Braeken for their willingness to join us on the editorial team to assure a text of high quality and as historically accurate as possible. Russell Shorto, the author of the bestseller *The Island at the Center of the World*, wrote a wonderful introduction to the main text.

The following authors contributed in particular to the substance of this travel guide, both in the main text and through inserts: David S. Cohen, Firth Haring Fabend, Donald R. Friary, Gary Hermalyn, Alicia Panko, Phillip Papas, Ruth Piwonka, Don Rittner, Roderic H. Blackburn, Elizabeth L. Bradley, Paul Finkelman, Hans Krabbendam, Walter Liedtke, Peter G. Rose, Eric Roth, Sean Sawyer, Annette Stott, Francis J. Sypher, Nicoline van der Sijs, David William Voorhees, Lori R. Weintrob. We owe most of the contents of this travel guide to them and to their often impressive local knowledge.

The continued strong commitment of the Citco Group of Companies, as well as that of Roald Smeets, was crucially important in creating this historical travel guide. We are also greatly indebted to all the donors without whose support this publication would never have been produced.

The Museum of the City of New York and its director, Susan Henshaw Jones; Sarah Henry; and, most notably, Kathleen Benson have been great supporters from an early stage and protected us from many pitfalls. We are very glad and proud that they decided to team up with us.

We also would like to thank Natalie Shivers for her crucial contribution as a copy-editor, Gwen Smith for the photo-editing, the design firm Pure+Applied for their creative design and layout, and Henk van Assen and Jiashan Wu for designing the maps. Grace-Yvette Gemmell contributed greatly with her research and fact-checking work. Finally, we would like to thank Dover Publications for believing in this project.

We are grateful to have been able to work with all of them in our efforts to highlight the Dutch legacy here!

Gajus Scheltema and Heleen Westerhuijs

CONTRIBUTORS

EDITORS

Hugo Gajus Scheltema: Dutch diplomat, Consul General of the Kingdom of The Netherlands in New York, 2007–2011; coordinated Dutch participation in the NY400 celebrations in New York, 2009; author of several publications on the history of art, archaeology, and political matters.

Heleen Westerhuijs: Independent scholar of Dutch architecture in the New World; master's degree in architectural history from the University of Amsterdam, 2009; she currently serves as director of Dutch New York projects for Citco Corporate, Inc., part of the Citco Group of Companies.

INTRODUCTION

Russell Shorto: Director, John Adams Institute, Amsterdam, The Netherlands; contributing writer, *New York Times Magazine*; author of several books, including *The Island at the Center of the World: The Epic Story of Dutch Manhattan and the Forgotten Colony That Shaped America*.

SPECIAL CONTRIBUTORS

Charles T. Gehring, PhD: Director, New Netherland Project, New York State Library; translator and editor of the 17th-century records of the Dutch West India Company colony centered in Manhattan.

Jaap Jacobs, PhD: Independent scholar; curatorial consultant for the Museum of the City of New York's 2009 exhibition *Amsterdam/New Amsterdam: The Worlds of Henry Hudson*; author of several books, including *The Colony of New Netherland: A Dutch Colony in Seventeenth Century America;* currently at work on a biography of Petrus Stuyvesant.

CONTRIBUTORS TO THE MAIN TEXT

David Steven Cohen, PhD: Former senior research associate and director, Ethnic History Program, New Jersey Historical Commission; former assistant professor of history, Rutgers University; author of six books, including *The Dutch-American Farm*.

Firth Haring Fabend, PhD: Historian; novelist; author of several books, including *A Dutch Family in the Middle Colonies, 1660–1800; Tappan: 300 Years, 1686–1986*; and *Zion on the Hudson: Dutch New York and New Jersey in the Age of Revivals*.

Donald R. Friary, PhD: President, Colonial Society of Massachusetts; Principal, History for Hire, Salem, Massachusetts.

Gary Hermalyn, PhD: Executive director, Bronx County Historical Society; president, History of New York City Project; associate editor, *The Encyclopedia of New York City*; author of *Morris High School and the Creation of the New York City Public High School System.*

Phillip Papas, PhD: Associate professor of history, Union County College; author of *That Ever Loyal Island: Staten Island and the American Revolution;* co-author, with Lori R. Weintrob, of *Port Richmond* and *The Other New York: The American Revolution beyond New York City, 1763–1787.*

Ruth Piwonka: Independent scholar; historian; author of *A Portrait of Livingston Manor, 1686–1850* and *Wooden Churches: Columbia County Legacy;* co-author (with Roderic Blackburn) of *Remembrance of Patria: Dutch Arts and Culture in Colonial America, 1609–1776* and *A Visible Heritage: Columbia County, New York: A History in Art and Architecture.*

Don Rittner: Schenectady County Historian; Schenectady City Historian; educator; publisher of *Skenectada,* a quarterly newsletter.

Sean Sawyer, PhD: Lecturer, master of arts program in decorative arts and design, Cooper-Hewitt National Design Museum/Parsons, The New School for Design; executive director, the Royal Oak Foundation

AUTHORS OF INSERTS

Roderic H. Blackburn: Author of *Dutch Colonial Homes in America;* co-author (with Ruth Piwonka) of *Remembrance of Patria: Dutch Arts and Culture in Colonial America 1609–1776;* and *A Visible Heritage: Columbia County, New York: History in Art and Architecture.*

Elizabeth L. Bradley, PhD: Deputy director of the Cullman Center for Scholars and Writers, the New York Public Library; author of *Knickerbocker: The Myth Behind New York*; editor of *Washington Irving's A History of New York*; contributor to *The Encyclopedia of New York City.*

Robert Braeken: Curator, Citco Group of Companies; cartographic consultant for the Museum of the City of New York's 2009 exhibition *Amsterdam/New Amsterdam: The Worlds of Henry Hudson.*

Paul Finkelman: President William McKinley Distinguished Professor of Law and Public Policy and senior fellow, Government Law Center, Albany Law School; author of more than 100 scholarly articles and more than 20 books.

Hans Krabbendam, PhD: Assistant director, Roosevelt Study Center, Middleburg, The Netherlands; Honorary Research Fellow, Hope College, Holland, MI; co-editor of *European Journal of American Studies*; author of *Freedom on the Horizon: Dutch Immigration to America, 1840–1940.*

Walter Liedtke, PhD: Curator of European paintings, the Metropolitan Museum of Art; author of several books, including: *Architectural Painting in Delft*; *Rembrandt/Not Rembrandt*; *The Royal Horse and Rider: Painting, Sculpture and Horsemanship*; *Vermeer: The Complete Paintings; Vermeer and the Delft School; Vermeer and His Contemporaries: A View of Delft*.

Peter G. Rose: Food historian; 2002 Alice P. Kenney Award winner; author of *The Sensible Cook: Dutch Foodways in the Old and the New World; Foods of the Hudson: A Seasonal Sampling of the Region's Bounty; Food, Drink and Celebrations of the Hudson Valley Dutch*; and *Summer Pleasures, Winter Pleasures: A Hudson Valley Cookbook*.

Eric Roth: Executive director, Historic Huguenot Street, New Paltz, New York; author of *For the Village: The Story of Huguenot Street*.

Annette Stott, PhD: Director, School of Art and Art History, and associate professor, art history and women's studies, University of Denver; author of *Holland Mania: The Unknown Dutch Period in American Art and Culture*; co-editor of *Going Dutch: The Dutch Presence in America, 1609–2009*.

Francis J. Sypher Jr., PhD: Editor of: *Liber A of the Collegiate Churches of New York, 1628–1700; The Charter of the Reformed Protestant Dutch Church of the City of New York; Minutes of Coroners Proceedings, City and County of New York, John Burnet, Coroner, 1748–1758*; translator of the Collegiate Church archives.

Nicoline van der Sijs, PhD: Linguist; etymologist; author of several books, including *Cookies, Coleslaw, and Stoops: The Influence of Dutch on the North American Languages*; winner of the ANV-Visser Nederlandia Prijs; winner of the Prijs voor de Geesteswetenschappen, Prins Bernard Cultuur fonds.

David William Voorhees, PhD: Director, Jacob Leisler Papers Project, New York University; trustee emeritus, the Holland Society of New York; editor of *de Halve Maen*, a quarterly scholarly journal devoted to New Netherland studies.

Lori R. Weintrob, PhD: Associate professor of history and department chair, Wagner College; director, Project Pericles, a program emphasizing civic learning and participatory democracy.

INDEX